EPISTEMOLOGY, A SYSTEMATIC OVERVIEW

ISBN: 978-1-326-11380-3

Copyright © 2014 Andreas Sofroniou.

Copyright © 2014 Andreas Sofroniou

EPISTEMOLOGY, A SYSTEMATIC OVERVIEW

ISBN: 978-1-326-11380-3

CONTENTS   *PAGE*

1. BACKGROUND AND MEANING   5

1.1 MEANING   5
1.2 PHILOSOPHY   5
1.3 METAPHYSICS   8
1.4 EPISTEMOLOGY   9
1.5 PHILOSOPHICAL THEORY OF KNOWLEDGE   10
1.6 SCIENCE, PHILOSOPHY OF   10
1.7 ANALYTIC PHILOSOPHY   12
1.8 PERCEPTION (IN PHILOSOPHY)   13
1.9 SUBSTANCE   13
1.10 PRAGMATISM   15
1.11 EXISTENTIALISM   15
1.12 SCEPTICISM   16
1.13 RATIONALISM   17
1.14 *A PRIORI AND A POSTERIORI*   17
1.15 NATIVISM   18
1.16 EMPIRICISM   18
1.17 VERIFICATIONISM (in philosophy)   19
1.18 HEIDEGGER, MARTIN (1889-1976)   20
1.19 ONTOLOGY   20
1.20 INDIAN THOUGHT   20

2. APPLICATION OF EPISTEMOLOGY   23

2.1 PRACTICAL APPLICATIONS   23
2.2 COMMON APPLICATIONS   23
2.3 PROPOSITIONAL KNOWLEDGE   26
2.4 BELIEF   27
2.5 TRUTH   27
2.6 JUSTIFICATION   28
2.7 PROPOSITIONS   29
2.8 EDMUND GETTIER   29
2.9 RESPONSES TO GETTIER   31
2.10 INFALLIBILISM, INDEFEASIBILITY   31

2

2.11 RELIABILISM   32
2.12 EXTERNALISM AND INTERNALISM   33
2.13 VALUE PROBLEM, THE   35
2.14 ACQUIRING KNOWLEDGE   36
2.15 ANALYTIC–SYNTHETIC DISTINCTION   38

3. TENDENCIES WITHIN EPISTEMOLOGY   39

3.1 HISTORICAL   39
3.2 EMPIRICISM   39
3.3 IDEALISM   39
3.4 RATIONALISM   40
3.5 CONSTRUCTIVISM   40
3.6 REGRESS PROBLEM, THE   41
3.7 RESPONSE TO THE REGRESS PROBLEM   41
3.8 INFINITISM   41
3.9 FOUNDATIONALISM   42
3.10 COHERENTISM   42
3.11 FOUNDHERENTISM   43
3.12 SCEPTICISM   44
3.13 DEVELOPMENTS FROM SCEPTICISM   44
3.14 EPISTEMIC CULTURE   45

4. KNOWLEDGE AND JUSTIFIED BELIEF   46

4.1 NARROW DEFINITION   46
4.2 SOURCES OF KNOWLEDGE & JUSTIFICATION   46
4.3 PERCEPTION (AS IN PHILOSOPHY)   47
4.4 INTROSPECTION   49
4.5 MEMORY   51
4.6 REASON   52
4.7 TESTIMONY   54
4.8 VIRTUE EPISTEMOLOGY   55
4.9 NATURALISTIC EPISTEMOLOGY   56
4.10 RELIGIOUS EPISTEMOLOGY   57
4.11 MORAL EPISTEMOLOGY   58

4.12 SOCIAL EPISTEMOLOGY	59
4.13 FEMINIST EPISTEMOLOGY	60
5. EPISTEMOLOGICAL LITERATURE	**61**
5.1 LIMITS OF HUMAN KNOWLEDGE.	61
5.2 STUDY OF KNOWLEDGE	61
5.3 REFLECTION-CORRESPONDENCE THEORY	62
5.4 RATIONALISM AND EMPIRICISM	63
5.5 PRAGMATICS	64
5.6 EVOLUTIONARY EPISTEMOLOGY	65
5.7 REPLICATED KNOWLEDGE	66
5.8 ANARCHISTIC, RELATIVISTIC ATTITUDE	68
6. EPISTEMOLOGY: CORE AREA OF PHILOSOPHY	**69**
6.1 NATURE, SOURCES AND LIMITS	69
6.2 FOUNDATIONALISM AND COHERENTISM	69
6.3 NATURALISTIC ANSWERS: CAUSES OF BELIEF	72
6.4 SCEPTICISM	73
6.5 RECENT DEVELOPMENTS IN EPISTEMOLOGY	75
7. SUMMING UP	**77**
7.1 EVALUATIONS	77
7.2 ANARCHISTIC OR RELATIVISTIC ATTITUDES	78
7.3 IMPORTANCE OF EPISTEMOLOGY	79
7.4 KEY ELEMENTS OF EPISTEMOLOGY	79
7.5 SYSTEMATIC OVERVIEW	80
INDEX	**81**
BIBLIOGRAPHY	**84**

1. BACKGROUND AND MEANING

1.1 MEANING

Epistemology (*ἐπιστήμη, episteme = science: the knowledge of, understanding* | and *λόγος, logos = the logical study of*) is the branch of philosophy concerned with the nature, scope and the application of scientific knowledge (*specific/natural sciences and social studies*).

Generally speaking, epistemology is also referred to as the 'theory of knowledge'. It questions what knowledge is and how it can be acquired and/or applied. To this extent, knowledge is pertinent to any given subject or entity.

Much of the debate in this field has focused on the philosophical analysis of the nature of knowledge and how it relates to connected notions such as truth, belief, and justification.

It has also been established that this theory of the method and the grounds of knowledge, is that branch of metaphysics which deals with the nature and validity of knowledge.

1.2 PHILOSOPHY

(**GREEK**, Φιλο = Friend of | Σωφια = Wisdom; **generally translated as '*LOVE OF WISDOM*'**)

The subject of philosophy is for the use of reason and argument in the search for truth and the nature of reality, especially of the causes and nature of things and of the principles governing existence, perception, human behaviour, and the material universe.

Philosophical activities can also be directed at understanding and clarifying the concepts, methods, and doctrines of other disciplines, or at reasoning itself and the concepts, methods, and doctrines of such general notions as truth, possibility,

5

knowledge (*epistemology*), necessity, existence (*ontology* and *metaphysics*), and proof.

Philosophy has many different areas, classified according to the subject-matter of the problems being addressed; thus, philosophy of mind is concerned with questions such as:

- 'How do the mental interact with the physical?'

- Philosophy of mathematics with questions such as 'what constitutes a proof?'

- Of religion ('does God exist?')

- Of science ('what constitutes good evidence for a hypothesis?')

- Of ethics; of politics; and indeed of any other discipline.

The first philosophers were also the first scientists, people who asked questions about the physical world and who attempted to answer them by observation and reasoning rather than by appealing to magic or to a God of some kind.

These people, known as the pre-Socratics, were the precursors of Socrates, Plato, and Aristotle, the three great philosophers who set the agenda for many of the philosophical questions debated today.

Philosophy regularly gives birth to new disciplines as one group of the questions it is trying to answer become amenable to study by the physical sciences.

Psychology, for example, is a discipline that is still in the process of separating itself from philosophy.

Great advances in scientific thinking have usually been accompanied by great advances in philosophical thinking.

6

For example, Galileo's work on the mechanics of planetary motion in the late 16th century was a motivating force in Descartes' work on knowledge and justification, while the physicist Albert Einstein (1879-1955) paid tribute to Hume as one of the philosophers whose work inspired his theory of relativity.

In the 20th century, the principal schools of philosophy are continental philosophy and logico-analytic philosophy. Within these principal schools, however, there are major divisions according to sides taken in the various great disputes of philosophy.

For example, until fairly recently it was a matter of great concern whether someone was a dualist or a monist--whether they believed that there are two different sorts of substance (the physical and the mental), or only one sort--either the physical (materialism) or the mental.

There are also major disputes about whether or not there are such things as 'innate ideas', concepts that are inborn rather than acquired through experience, and whether we can make sense of a world that is independent of us and our minds (realism) or whether the mind is in fact more fundamental than some extra-mental reality (idealism).

Rather than being empirical scientists, philosophers try to discern the logical form of the problems in which they are interested and to discover hidden fallacies or habits of mind which might be obscuring understanding. The only experiments indulged in by philosophers are thought experiments.

The interpretation of various doctrines in modern physics is currently of great interest to philosophers: at least one interpretation of the laws of quantum physics would invalidate some of the rules of classical logic. Moreover, advances in engineering, computing and psychology have

7

brought us close to the production of an artificial intelligence, a fact of interest not only to philosophers of mind, but one that introduces ethical questions of great importance.

Major areas in which philosophy can be applied to the problems of everyday life are moral and political philosophy, especially in medical ethics such as the prevention of conception and the enhancement of fertility.

In such cases very deep moral problems arise, the solutions to which require sustained and critical examination of what is right and what is wrong.

These investigations are usually carried out by interdisciplinary committees in which philosophers play a major part.

1.3 METAPHYSICS

(**Metaphysics** = Μεταφυσικα, Μετα τα Φυσικα = Meta ta Physica) is from Greek, 'the things after the physics', from the ordering of Aristotle's works).

This is the branch of philosophy which studies the most general categories and concepts which are presupposed in descriptions of us and the world. Examples are causality, substance, ontology, time, and reality.

Metaphysical questions have a very broad scope. Whereas the physical scientist might ask 'How does x cause y?' the metaphysician asks 'What does it mean for anything to cause anything else?' Whereas the chemist might investigate particular substances, the metaphysician asks what it means to be a substance, and whether there is one basic substance, or many.

Metaphysical questions can become the subject of more specialised philosophical inquiry. We can ask whether our

8

actions are subject to causality, which gives rise to the problem of free will.

Also the question of whether our mental experiences involve a separate substance from body is a major issue in the philosophy of mind. Although metaphysics dates back to the ancient Greeks, there have been occasions on which its status as a legitimate inquiry have been questioned.

The rise of science in the 17th century led to attempts by philosophers such as Hume and Locke to limit the claims of metaphysics, and earlier this century scientifically minded philosophers such as the logical positivists claimed that metaphysical assertions were meaningless.

1.4 EPISTEMOLOGY

(Derived from Greek; *epistēme* meaning 'Science/Knowledge' and *logos* meaning 'Reason/Study of').

Epistemology, the study of knowledge translates the German concept Wissenschaftslehre, which was used by Fichte and Bolzano for different projects before it was taken up again by Husserl.

J.F. Ferrier coined the word on the model of 'ontology', to designate that branch of philosophy which aims to discover the meaning of knowledge, and called it the 'true beginning' of philosophy.

French philosophers then gave the term *épistémologie* a narrower meaning as 'theory of knowledge *[théorie de la connaissance]*.' Thus Émile Meyerson opened his *Identity and Reality*, written in 1908, with the remark that the word 'is becoming current' as equivalent to 'the philosophy of the sciences *[philosophie des sciences]*.'

9

1.5 PHILOSOPHICAL THEORY OF KNOWLEDGE

It is generally assumed that the difference between a belief which makes a genuine claim to knowledge, and one which is a mere statement of opinion is that the former can somehow be justified.

Epistemology can be regarded as the investigation of what constitutes that justification, and how, or whether, it can be attained. Scepticism is the position which holds that justification, and hence knowledge, is not possible.

Traditionally conflicting theories about knowledge have been rationalism, which claims that ultimate justification for our beliefs is to be found in reason (*a priori*), and empiricism, which argues that it is to be found in our sense-experiences. The traditional debate, then, has concerned the nature of the foundation of knowledge.

More recently, however, attention has been focused on the structure of knowledge, that is, how our true beliefs are related to one another. The assumption that knowledge has to have a starting-point in any sort of foundation has been questioned by the Coherence Theory of Knowledge, which suggests, instead, that a belief is justified to the extent to which it fits in, or coheres with, all our other beliefs.

1.6 SCIENCE, PHILOSOPHY OF

This refers to the investigation of the concepts and methods of the natural and social sciences.

There are two major themes. Historically the most important is the realism debate which dates back to the time of the pioneer astronomer scientists Galileo (1564-1642) and Copernicus (1473-1543) and is concerned with the interpretation of scientific theories.

10

The question is whether these theories should be regarded as true descriptions of the world (scientific realism) or whether they are rather instruments which are not literally true, but simply useful in that they enable us to make successful predictions about immediately observable phenomena (instrumentalism).

A more recent debate concerning the nature of scientific progress is the rationality debate, which asks how we can characterize the 'scientific method', or even whether such a single, universal method can be identified. Both debates have strong links with epistemology, the theory of knowledge.

On the question of scientific rationality we can ask what sort of justification there can be for the choice of one scientific theory over another. In the realism issue, we can ask whether we have adequate justification for regarding scientific statements as literally true. A further question is the relationship between the natural sciences (such as physics and chemistry) and the social sciences (such as economics and sociology).

Should they be regarded as close enough to share the same methods (as in Comte's positivism)? Or are the methods of the natural sciences inappropriate for the subject-matter of the social sciences? Do the natural and social sciences even have the same aim? It has been argued that the aim of natural science is prediction and control of natural processes, whereas the aim of the social sciences is to understand human behaviour.

The question of reductionism plays a role here: can sociology be reduced to psychology, and psychology in turn to a more physically grounded neuroscience? Or are social and psychological processes irreducible?

11

1.7 ANALYTIC PHILOSOPHY

This is a broad movement in the 20th-century philosophy, influential chiefly in Austria, the UK, and the USA, which regards central philosophical problems as primarily demanding clarification or analysis of such notions as meaning, truth, and necessity.

Although analytical philosophy is a loosely unified tradition, rather than a specific doctrine, there has been broad agreement on some specific matters.

First, philosophy is a distinctive kind of enquiry, which employs methods different from those of the natural or social sciences; additionally, unlike, for instance, biology or economics, it is not addressed to any distinctive realm of facts. Philosophy does not seek to construct theories which build upon or add to our knowledge of the world, but to clarify the knowledge and beliefs we already have.

Secondly, this clarification is to be achieved by analysis of the language in which our non-philosophical, common-sense, or scientific knowledge is expressed. This framework leaves ample room for internal divisions.

There is, for instance, disagreement between Russell's view that this kind of clarification will yield answers to the traditional questions of metaphysics and epistemology, and Wittgenstein's contention that such questions are the products of confusions which the careful analysis of language will enable us to avoid.

A related dispute concerns whether philosophical analysis can itself be conducted in a systematic way, using the tools and techniques of mathematical logic, as the logical positivists held, or whether resolution of philosophical problems demands piecemeal attention to specific areas of ordinary language. In general, workers in the tradition are suspicious of system-building, priding themselves on rigour of argument and clarity of expression.

Critics of the tradition say it is arid, concerned with minute points of detail, and ignore the major philosophical problems.

1.8 PERCEPTION (IN PHILOSOPHY)

Perception is the sensory process by means of which we get knowledge of the external world. The philosophical problem of perception is epistemological: how are we to justify perceptual claims to knowledge? This question is not answered by psychology, which already assumes the existence of an external world.

The main difficulty consists in showing why we should trust our perceptual experiences, given that we have apparently identical kinds of experience which are illusory, such as dream and hallucination.

Philosophical theories of perception include representational realism, which says that external objects are hypothesised in order to explain and match our experiences, and phenomenalism, according to which external objects are in fact nothing but bundles of experiences.

1.9 SUBSTANCE

This is a philosophical term meaning roughly a thing, or independently existing thing.

Philosophical questions about substance are questions about what things, or kinds of things, fundamentally exist. Aristotle characterised a substance grammatically as 'what is neither said of, nor in a subject'.

13

So, for instance, in 'Johnnie is running', *running* is said of, or said to be a feature of, Johnnie, but Johnnie cannot in this sense be said of anything else.

Things can in turn be said of *running*, as in 'running is healthy', but here it seems clear that what are ultimately being spoken of are people, individual things, or substances, which run: people who run tend to be healthy.

Again, Johnnie is something independent in a way that *running* is not: Johnnie can exist without *running*, but *running* cannot exist unless someone runs. As well as this primary sense of substance, Aristotle recognised a secondary sense in which it answers the question *what* something is: ' Johnnie is running' tells us what Johnnie happens to be doing, but ' Johnnie is a man' tells us what kind of thing Johnnie fundamentally is.

Primary substances are thus the individual things the world fundamentally contains, and secondary substances the basic kinds into which these things fall. In its long history the notion of substance has been modified and applied in various areas of philosophy.

The rationalist Descartes made the notion central to his epistemology: true knowledge of the world must rest on insight into the essential natures of the basic kinds of things it contains, in Descartes' dualist philosophy, minds and material things.

From Locke onwards empiricists, doubting our ability to achieve this insight, have been wary of the notion of substance. Even so, Locke's philosophy reluctantly casts substance in various roles: whatever it is that has the various properties we speak of in describing the world, or what lies behind and causes our diverse perceptions of it.

14

That nothing can fill all the roles ascribed to substance perhaps explain why the notion has frequently fallen into philosophical disrepute.

1.10 PRAGMATISM

A US philosophical tradition originally developed by Charles Peirce (1839-1914) and then extended by, amongst others, James and Dewey.

Its main claims, easily caricatured, are that statements only have meaning to the extent that they can affect our actions, and that truth is, ultimately, what works for a scientifically sophisticated community.

It thus has strong affinities with, but is more subtle than, positivism. Although pilloried by Russell, it has had a powerful influence on many modern philosophers, especially those drawn towards coherence theories of truth and epistemology.

1.11 EXISTENTIALISM

Existentialism is a movement in mid-20th-century continental philosophy.

In the post-war years it gripped the imagination of many thinkers, writers, and artists. Its appeal lay partly in its ability to reflect the alienation and experience of atrocity in 20th-century Europe.

Existentialist philosophers speculated about the nature of reality, but subordinated traditional metaphysical and epistemological questions to an anthropocentric perspective, in which there takes place a dramatic, often tragic, confrontation between man and the world.

Existentialist thought tends to disparage scientific knowledge, particularly psychology, in so far as it claims to be a science, and to insist on the absence of objective values, stressing instead the reality and significance of human freedom.

Influenced by Kierkegaard, existentialism gave rise to a tradition of Christian existentialism, but the best-known exponents of existentialism in its atheistic form are Heidegger and Sartre. Existentialism cannot be easily identified with any single set of philosophical ideas.

It took contemporary inspiration from Husserl's phenomenology, but derived also from various sources in 19th-century philosophy, including Nietzsche and Kierkegaard, whose conception of the 'individual' may be regarded as a prototype for the existentialist view of the human being as solitary, contingent, and self-creating.

1.12 SCEPTICISM

This term refers to any philosophical position which maintains that our beliefs about a certain subject-matter cannot be justified.

Epistemology, the philosophical theory of knowledge, has often been regarded as the search for an effective answer to scepticism. Scepticism can be either global or local. Global scepticism is concerned with all our beliefs about the external world, and claims that we can have no knowledge of the way that the world really is.

Local scepticism is more specific, and only claims that beliefs in a certain area, such as ethics, cannot be justified. Local scepticism can be used as a way of showing that commonly accepted beliefs about a subject cannot be maintained because they lead to a sceptical conclusion. Hume, for example, used scepticism in this way in his discussion of induction.

16

1.13 RATIONALISM

A broad philosophical position characterised by the claim that reason is, in some way, a source of knowledge.

This claim can mean either that reason provides us with *a priori* concepts (or innate ideas) which can give the content of knowledge, or, more simply, that sense-experience gives the content which then has to be corrected, and justified, by reason.

Rationalist is the common label for 17th-century continental philosophers such as Descartes, Leibniz, and Spinoza. In the works of these authors, much emphasis is put on systematic justification, and mathematics, especially geometry, is often taken to be the template of an ideal rationalist epistemology.

Traditionally, rationalism stands opposed to empiricism, in which experience provides us with all of our concepts, and is the ultimate source of justification of knowledge claims. Philosophers such as Kant attempted to synthesise the insights of the two.

1.14 *A PRIORI AND A POSTERIORI*

A PRIORI is the term from epistemology meaning knowledge or concepts which can be gained independently of all experience.

It is contrasted with *a posteriori* knowledge, in which experience plays an essential role.

Statements such as 'all bachelors are unmarried' are known as analytic truths: the concept 'bachelor' and the concept 'unmarried' are inter-definable.

Analytic truths, then, provide one form of *a priori* knowledge.

17

For example, simply because of the meaning of the concept 'bachelor', we know *a priori* that if John is a bachelor, then John has no wife.

On the other hand, knowledge of whether John is a bachelor or not would be *a posteriori* because its discovery requires some form of empirical investigation.

The extent of *a priori* knowledge is much debated. Rationalists and others, including Kant, argue that we can have substantial *a priori* knowledge. Empiricist philosophies, though, generally limit *a priori* knowledge to that derivable from analytic truths.

1.15 NATIVISM

A school of philosophical thought according to which at least some of our concepts are innate, such that they are prior to and (sometimes) independent of our sense experience. Famous nativists were Plato, Descartes, and Kant.

Nativism was eschewed by the British empiricists Locke, Berkeley, and Hume, who believed that all our concepts are acquired through experience and that at birth our minds are *tabulae rasae* ('clean slates').

The dilemma facing nativists is similar to that of the nature-nurture debate, because even if some concepts are innate they may need to be triggered by experience, and it is very difficult to disentangle the contribution of experience from whatever was innate.

1.16 EMPIRICISM

The term empiricism is a doctrine in the theory of knowledge, which stresses the primacy of sense-experience over reason in the acquisition and justification of knowledge. It thus stands opposed to rationalism, and limits a priori knowledge.

Although explicit empiricist notions can be found in medieval philosophy, and perhaps even earlier, its main impetus was gained during the 17th-century revolution in physics, when adherence to empiricist controls was advocated as an antidote to scientifically unproductive metaphysical speculation.

The demand for philosophy to be responsive to the needs of science is a theme that has been invariant through the empiricist tradition from Locke and Hume to Russell and the logical positivists, and is present also in pragmatism.

1.17 VERIFICATIONISM (IN PHILOSOPHY)

The view that the meaning of a proposition is its method of verification, the procedure by which its truth or falsity can be determined by observation or experience. Verificationism was adopted by the logical positivists and was strongly influenced by the empiricist tradition.

The verificationist claim resulted in many, if not all, of the propositions of metaphysics being rendered meaningless: as they cannot be verified, they cannot have meaning. It also resulted in the propositions of mathematics and of logic (which are of course consistent with all observations) being seen as meaningful only in the sense of being tautologies; they tell us nothing and merely show us how things are.

As any non-tautological proposition that cannot be verified by observation is deemed meaningless, this renders all the propositions of ethics and of aesthetics meaningless too, and useful only as expressions of emotion or exclamations.

A major problem for verificationism is that it puts the meaning of all scientific generalisations in jeopardy because these cannot be conclusively verified by observation.

1.18 HEIDEGGER, MARTIN (1889-1976)

German philosopher, a student of Husserl and important contributor to existentialism. In his central work, *Being and Time* (1927), Heidegger attempted to return philosophy to contemplation of what he took to be the outstandingly important question, 'What is being?'

Though he never claimed to be able to answer this question, Heidegger evolved a new philosophical vocabulary in which traditional metaphysics and epistemology gave way to an analysis of the distinctive features of human existence (referred to by Heidegger as *Dasein*, 'being there'). Heidegger's philosophical achievement is sometimes argued to be tainted by his involvement with Nazism.

1.19 ONTOLOGY

This is the philosophical study of the nature of being.

Although this can be taken to be the study of what it is for anything to exist at all, as in Heidegger's work, ontological questions are also concerned with what, in particular, exists.

Thus our common-sense ontology would include the material objects with which we interact (such as trees, tables, and mountains), but should it also contain abstract mathematical entities (sets and numbers) or the sub-atomic entities of the theoretical sciences (such as protons and muons)? Closely linked is the question of reductionism. For example, can minds be reduced to bodies, or mathematics to logic?

A major question is how we are to decide ontological issues. Ockham's razor, the principle, formulated by William of Ockham in about 1340, that we should not multiply entities beyond necessity, is generally thought of as a principle in the theory of knowledge or epistemology, and was used as such by

20

Russell. But in recent philosophy this has also often been linked to questions of meaning, as in logical positivism.

1.20 INDIAN THOUGHT

Modern Indian thought takes three interrelated forms depending on the style and concerns of its proponents. First, traditionalists, usually called *pundits*, trained in Sanskrit, attempt to preserve the classical tradition through commentaries and discussions chiefly in social and religious contexts, and are generally not much concerned with contemporary philosophical developments in the West and elsewhere.

They are not interested in interacting with other social groups and tend not to be known outside the circle of interested Sanskrit scholars. They preserve most clearly the linguistic tradition of classical Sanskrit learning. Secondly, ideological thinkers who, especially in the 19th and early 20th centuries, responded to Western denigration of Indian moral and intellectual values by appealing to the greatness of significant past Indian thinkers and texts.

Their primary aim was to develop an understanding of India's past which allowed them to claim that it had an intellectual tradition, but they themselves did not construct philosophical systems. They were often social activists and reformers.

Others, such as Mahatma Gandhi (1869-1948) and Jawaharlal Nehru (1889-1964), are often considered to be thinkers in this sense because of their ideological views about the achievements and potential of Indian culture.

The third and final category includes academic thinkers who follow largely Western models in addressing tightly focused issues with the apparatus of technical terminology. Though they accept that there is an unavoidable use of Western modes of discussion, especially because of the predominant use of English and German, they argue that their reconstructed

21

understanding of the tradition is merely a contemporary method of preserving the classical tradition, and as such, quintessentially Indian.

The authoritative translation and interpretation of classical Sanskrit texts is an important element of this modern study and several Western scholars have contributed to this field.

Examples of such Indian philosophers are:

- K. Coomaraswamy (1877-1947), who sought to develop a perennial philosophy whose metaphysical and aesthetic bases would nourish the continuity of different traditional cultures;

- S. Radhakrishnan, best-known of modern thinkers, who wrote on both his own interpretation of Advaita Vedanta, and on comparative analyses of Indian and Western ideas, especially the supposed parallel between Advaita and idealism;

- SriAurobindo Ghosh (1872-1950), whose later philosophy combined with his saintly character to produce a vision of the spiritual and moral anticipation of all humanity;

- K. C. Bhattacharya, an authentically modern thinker whose primary aim was to develop an entire system of thought which used both Western elements like the philosophy of Kant and Hegel, and Indian elements like Advaita Vedanta (which is the dominant paradigm of modern reconstruction);

- K. Motilal (1936-91), who employed Western analytic methods in reconstructing classical Indian epistemology, theory of language, and metaphysics, in order to contribute to contemporary debate in these areas in the West.

22

2. APPLICATION OF EPISTEMOLOGY

2.1 Practical Applications

Epistemology is particularly commonly employed in issues of law where proof of guilt or innocence may be required, or when it must be determined whether a person knew a particular fact before taking a specific action (e.g., whether an action was premeditated).

Another practical application is to the design of user interfaces.

For example, the skills, rules, and knowledge taxonomy of human behaviour has been used by designers to develop systems that are compatible with multiple "ways of knowing":

    i.   Abstract analytic reasoning,

    ii.   Experience-based 'gut feelings', and

    iii.   'Craft' sensorimotor skills.

2.2 COMMON APPLICATIONS

Other common applications of epistemology include:

➤ ARCHAEOLOGY

➤ ARTIFICIAL INTELLIGENCE

➤ BEHAVIOURAL NEUROSCIENCE

➤ COGNITIVE SCIENCE

➤ COMPUTING

➤ CYBERNETIC EPISTEMOLOGY

➤ EASTERN EPISTEMOLOGY

- ECONOMICS
- EDUCATION THEORY
- EDUCATIONAL TECHNOLOGY
- EPISTEMOLOGICAL RUPTURE
- EVOLUTIONARY EPISTEMOLOGY
- FEMINIST EPISTEMOLOGY
- FORMAL EPISTEMOLOGY
- GÖDEL'S INCOMPLETENESS THEOREMS
- INFORMATION GATHERING
- INFORMATION TECHNOLOGY
- INTELLIGENCE GATHERING
- KNOWLEDGE MANAGEMENT
- LAW
- MATHEMATICS
- MEDICINE (DIAGNOSIS OF DISEASE)
- META-EPISTEMOLOGY
- METHODOLOGY
- METHODS OF OBTAINING KNOWLEDGE
- MONOPOLIES OF KNOWLEDGE
- MUSIC
- NEUROLOGY
- NOÖLOGY

➢ **PARTICIPATORY EPISTEMOLOGY**

➢ **PHILOLOGY AND LITERATURE**

➢ **PROBLEM OF OTHER MINDS**

➢ **PRODUCT TESTING**

➢ **PROPOSITIONAL KNOWLEDGE**

➢ **PSYCHOLOGY**

➢ **REFORMED EPISTEMOLOGY**

➢ **RELIGION**

➢ **SCIENTIFIC METHOD**

➢ **SELF-EVIDENCE**

➢ **SEMIOTICS**

➢ **SOCIAL EPISTEMOLOGY**

➢ **SOCIOLOGY OF KNOWLEDGE**

➢ **SOFTWARE TESTING**

➢ **SUBJECT–OBJECT PROBLEM**

➢ **TECHNOLOGY**

➢ **TESTIMONY**

➢ **UNCERTAINTY PRINCIPLE**

➢ **VIRTUE**

2.3 PROPOSITIONAL KNOWLEDGE

Propositional Knowledge entails that, knowledge how, and knowledge by acquaintance.

In epistemology (in general), the kind of knowledge usually discussed is propositional knowledge, also known as "knowledge that." This is distinguished from "knowledge how" and "acquaintance-knowledge".

For example: in mathematics, it is known *that* $2 + 2 = 4$, but there is also knowing *how* to add two numbers and knowing a *person* (e.g., oneself), *place* (e.g., one's hometown), *thing* (e.g., cars), or *activity* (e.g., addition).

Some philosophers think there is an important distinction between "knowing that," "knowing how," and "acquaintance-knowledge," with epistemology being primarily concerned with the first of these.

In his paper *On Denoting* and his later book *Problems of Philosophy* Bertrand Russell stressed the distinction between "knowledge by description" and "knowledge by acquaintance". Gilbert Ryle is also credited with stressing the distinction between knowing how and knowing that in *The Concept of Mind.*

In *Personal Knowledge,* Michael Polanyi argues for the epistemological relevance of knowledge how and knowledge that; using the example of the act of balance involved in riding a bicycle, he suggests that the theoretical knowledge of the physics involved in maintaining a state of balance cannot substitute for the practical knowledge of how to ride, and that it is important to understand how both are established and grounded.

26

This position is essentially Ryle's, who argued that a failure to acknowledge the distinction between knowledge that and knowledge how leads to infinite regress.

In recent times, some epistemologists (Sosa, Greco, Kvanvig, and Zagzebski) and Duncan Pritchard have argued that epistemology should evaluate people's "properties" (i.e., intellectual virtues) and not just the properties of propositions or of propositional mental attitudes.

2.4 BELIEF

In common speech, a "statement of belief" is typically an expression of faith and/or trust in a person, power or other entity — while it includes such traditional views, epistemology is also concerned with what we believe. This includes 'the' truth, and everything else we accept as true for ourselves from a cognitive point of view.

2.5 TRUTH

Whether someone's belief is true is not a prerequisite for (its) belief. On the other hand, if something is actually *known*, then it categorically cannot be false.

For example, if a person believes that a bridge is safe enough to support him, and attempts to cross it, but the bridge then collapses under his weight, it could be said that he *believed* that the bridge was safe but that his belief was mistaken.

It would *not* be accurate to say that he *knew* that the bridge was safe, because plainly it was not. By contrast, if the bridge actually supported his weight, then he might say that he had believed that the bridge was safe, whereas now, after proving it to himself (by crossing it), he *knows* it was safe.

Epistemologists argue over whether belief is the proper truth-bearer. Some would rather describe knowledge as a system of justified true propositions, and others as a system of justified true sentences. Plato, in his Gorgias, argues that belief is the most commonly invoked truth-bearer.

2.6 JUSTIFICATION

In many of Plato's dialogues, such as the *Meno* and, in particular, the *Theaetetus*, Socrates considers a number of theories as to what knowledge is, the last being that knowledge is true belief that has been "given an account of" (meaning explained or defined in some way).

According to the theory that knowledge is justified true belief, in order to know that a given proposition is true, one must not only believe the relevant true proposition, but one must also have a good reason for doing so. One implication of this would be that no one would gain knowledge just by believing something that happened to be true.

For example, an ill person with no medical training, but with a generally optimistic attitude, might believe that he will recover from his illness quickly. Nevertheless, even if this belief turned out to be true, the patient would not have *known* that he would get well since his belief lacked justification.

The definition of knowledge as justified true belief was widely accepted until the 1960s. At this time, a paper written by the American philosopher Edmund Gettier provoked major widespread discussion.

2.7 PROPOSITIONS

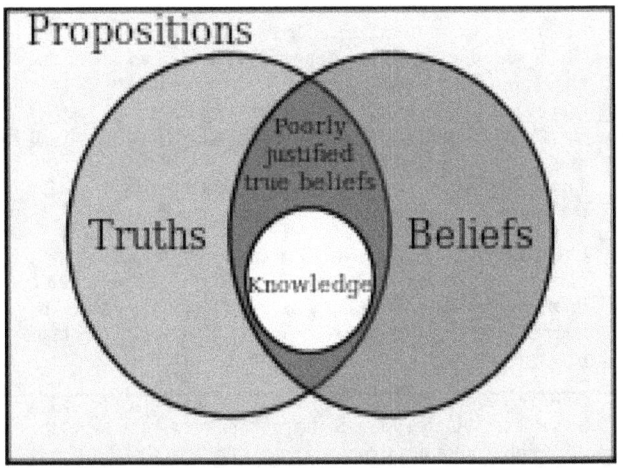

Euler diagram representing a definition of knowledge.

2.8 EDMUND GETTIER

Edmund Gettier is best known for a short paper entitled 'Is Justified True Belief Knowledge?' published in 1963, which called into question the theory of knowledge that had been dominant among philosophers for thousands of years. In a few pages, Gettier argued that there are situations in which one's belief may be justified and true, yet fail to count as knowledge.

That is, Gettier contended that while justified belief in a true proposition is necessary for that proposition to be known, it is

29

not sufficient. As in the diagram, a true proposition can be believed by an individual (purple region) but still not fall within the "knowledge" category (yellow region).

According to Gettier, there are certain circumstances in which one does not have knowledge, even when all of the above conditions are met. Gettier proposed two thought experiments, which have come to be known as "Gettier cases," as counter-examples to the classical account of knowledge. One of the cases involves two men, Smith and Jones, who are awaiting the results of their applications for the same job.

Each man has ten coins in his pocket. Smith has excellent reasons to believe that Jones will get the job and, furthermore, knows that Jones has ten coins in his pocket (he recently counted them). From this Smith infers, "the man who will get the job has ten coins in his pocket."

However, Smith is unaware that he also has ten coins in his own pocket. Furthermore, Smith, not Jones, is going to get the job. While Smith has strong evidence to believe that Jones will get the job, he is wrong.

Smith has a justified true belief that a man with ten coins in his pocket will get the job; however, according to Gettier, Smith does not *know* that a man with ten coins in his pocket will get the job, because Smith's belief is "...true by virtue of the number of coins in *Jones's* pocket, while Smith does not know how many coins are in Smith's pocket, and bases his belief...on a count of the coins in Jones's pocket, whom he falsely believes to be the man who will get the job."

These cases fail to be knowledge because the subject's belief is justified, but only happens to be true by virtue of luck. In other words, he made the correct choice (in this case predicting an outcome) for the wrong reasons.

This example is similar to those often given when discussing belief and truth, wherein a person's belief of what will happen can coincidentally be correct without his or her having the actual knowledge to base it on.

2.9 RESPONSES TO GETTIER

The responses to Gettier have been varied. Usually, they have involved substantial attempts to provide a definition of knowledge different from the classical one, either by recasting knowledge as justified true belief with some additional fourth condition, or as something else altogether.

2.10 INFALLIBILISM, INDEFEASIBILITY

In one response to Gettier, the American philosopher Richard Kirkham has argued that the only definition of knowledge that could ever be immune to all counter-examples is the infallibilist one. To qualify as an item of knowledge, goes the theory, a belief must not only be true and justified, the justification of the belief must *necessitate* its truth. In other words, the justification for the belief must be infallible.

Yet another possible candidate for the fourth condition of knowledge is *indefeasibility*. Defeasibility theory maintains that there should be no overriding or defeating truths for the reasons that justify one's belief.

For example, suppose that person *S* believes he saw Tom Grabit steal a book from the library and uses this to justify the claim that Tom Grabit stole a book from the library.

A possible defeater or overriding proposition for such a claim could be a true proposition like, "Tom Grabit's identical twin Sam is currently in the same town as Tom." When no defeaters of one's justification exist, a subject would be epistemically justified.

31

The Indian philosopher B K Matilal has drawn on the Navya-Nyāya fallibilism tradition to respond to the Gettier problem. Nyaya theory distinguishes between *know p* and *know that one knows p* – these are different events, with different causal conditions.

The second level is a sort of implicit inference that usually follows immediately the episode of knowing p (knowledge *simpliciter*). The Gettier case is examined by referring to a view of Gangesha Upadhyaya (late 12th century), who takes any true belief to be knowledge; thus a true belief acquired through a wrong route may just be regarded as knowledge simpliciter on this view.

The question of justification arises only at the second level, when one considers the knowledgehood of the acquired belief. Initially, there is lack of uncertainty, so it becomes a true belief.

But at the very next moment, when the hearer is about to embark upon the venture of *knowing whether he knows p*, doubts may arise. "If, in some Gettier-like cases, I am wrong in my inference about the knowledgehood of the given occurrent belief (for the evidence may be pseudo-evidence), then I am mistaken about the truth of my belief – and this is in accordance with Nyaya fallibilism: not all knowledge - claims can be sustained."

2.11 RELIABILISM

Reliabilism has been a significant line of response to the Gettier problem among philosophers, originating with work by Alvin Goldman in the 1960s.

According to reliabilism, a belief is justified (or otherwise supported in such a way as to count towards knowledge) only if it is produced by processes that typically yield a sufficiently high ratio of true to false beliefs.

In other words, this theory states that a true belief counts as knowledge only if it is produced by a reliable belief-forming process.

Reliabilism has been challenged by Gettier cases.

Another argument that challenges reliabilism, like the Gettier cases (although it was not presented in the same short article as the Gettier cases), is the case of Henry and the barn façades.

In the thought experiment, a man, Henry, is driving along and sees a number of buildings that resemble barns. Based on his perception of one of these, he concludes that he has just seen barns. While he has seen one, and the perception he based his belief that the one he saw was of a real barn, all the other barn-like buildings he saw were façades.

Theoretically, Henry does not know that he has seen a barn, despite both his belief that he has seen one being true and his belief being formed on the basis of a reliable process (i.e. his vision), since he only acquired his true belief by accident.

2.12 EXTERNALISM AND INTERNALISM

Part of the debate over the nature of knowledge is a debate between epistemological externalists on the one hand, and epistemological internalists on the other.

Externalists hold that factors deemed "external", meaning outside of the psychological states of those who gain knowledge, can be conditions of knowledge.

For example, an externalist response to the Gettier problem is to say that, in order for a justified true belief to count as knowledge, there must be a link or dependency between the belief and the state of the external world. Usually this is understood to be a causal link.

Such causation, to the extent that it is "outside" the mind, would count as an external, knowledge-yielding condition. Internalists, on the other hand, assert that all knowledge-yielding conditions are within the psychological states of those who gain knowledge.

Though unfamiliar with the internalist/externalist debate himself, many point to René Descartes as an early example of the internalist path to justification. He wrote that, because the only method by which we perceive the external world is through our senses, and that, because the senses are not infallible, we should not consider our concept of knowledge to be infallible.

The only way to find anything that could be described as "indubitably true," he advocates would be to see things "clearly and distinctly". He argued that if there is an omnipotent, good being that made the world, then it is reasonable to believe that people are made with the ability to know. However, this does not mean that man's ability to know is perfect. God gave man the ability to know, but not omniscience. Descartes said that man must use his capacities for knowledge correctly and carefully through methodological doubt.

The dictum "Cogito ergo sum" (I think, therefore I am) is also commonly associated with Descartes' theory, because in his own methodological doubt, doubting everything he previously knew in order to start from a blank slate, the first thing that he could not logically bring himself to doubt was his own existence: "I do not exist" would be a contradiction in terms; the act of saying that one does not exist assumes that someone must be making the statement in the first place.

Though Descartes could doubt his senses, his body and the world around him, he could not deny his own existence, because he was able to doubt and must exist in order to do so.

34

Even if some "evil genius" were to be deceiving him, he would have to exist in order to be deceived.

This one sure point provided him with what he would call his Archimedean point, in order to further develop his foundation for knowledge. Simply put, Descartes' epistemological justification depended upon his indubitable belief in his own existence and his clear and distinct knowledge of God.

2.13 VALUE PROBLEM, THE

A formulation of the value problem in epistemology first occurs in Plato's Meno. The problem is to identify what is it about knowledge (if anything) that makes it more valuable than mere true belief, or that makes knowledge more valuable than a more minimal conjunction of its components on a particular analysis of knowledge.

The value problem re-emerged in the philosophical literature on epistemology in the twenty-first century following the rise of virtue epistemology in the 1980s, partly because of the obvious link with the concept of value in ethics.

The value problem has been presented as an argument against epistemic reliabilism by philosophers including Linda Zagzebski, Wayne Riggs and Richard Swinburne. Zagzebski gives a thought experiment to illustrate the unimportance of the belief being produced by a reliable process: imagine you go to a coffee machine and attempt to have it produce you a cup of coffee. The machine you use might reliably produce coffee, or it might not.

Imagine one machine had a 90% chance of producing you coffee while another only had a 40% chance. If you happen to choose the 40% chance machine and it produces you a cup of coffee, the fact that it does not *reliably* produce coffee does not change the value that the coffee has to you.

Similarly, if you have a true belief achieved through an unreliable process, Zagzebski argues that there's no particular reason that has *less* value than one produced through a reliable process. Advocates of virtue epistemology have argued that the value of knowledge comes from an internal relationship between the knower and the mental state of believing.

One of the more influential responses to the problem is that knowledge is not particularly valuable and is not what ought to be the main focus of epistemology. Instead, epistemologists ought to focus on other mental states, such as understanding.

2.14 ACQUIRING KNOWLEDGE

A priori and *a posteriori* knowledge

The nature of this distinction has been disputed by various philosophers; however, the terms may be roughly defined as follows:

> *A priori* knowledge is knowledge that is known independently of experience (that is, it is non-empirical, or arrived at beforehand, usually by reason). It will henceforth be acquired through anything that is independent from experience.

> *A posteriori* knowledge is knowledge that is known by experience (that is, it is empirical, or arrived at afterward).

A priori knowledge is a way of gaining knowledge without the need of experience. In Bruce Russell's article "A Priori Justification and Knowledge" he says that it is "knowledge based on a priori justification," which relies on intuition and the nature of these intuitions. A priori knowledge is often contrasted with posteriori knowledge, which is knowledge gained by experience.

A way to look at the difference between the two is through an example. Bruce Russell give two proposition in which the reader decides which one he believes more.

Option A: All crows are birds.

Option B: All crows are black.

If you believe option A, then you are a priori justified in believing it because you don't have to see a crow to know it's a bird.

If you believe in option B, then you are posteriori justified to believe it because you have seen many crows therefore knowing they are black.

He goes on to say that it does not matter if the statement is true or not, only that if you believe in one or the other that matters.

The idea of a priori knowledge is that it is based on intuition or rational insights. Laurence BonJour says in his article "The Structure of Empirical Knowledge", that a "rational insight is an immediate, non-inferential grasp, apprehension or 'seeing' that some proposition is necessarily true."

Going back to the crow example, by Laurence BonJour's definition the reason you would believe in option A is because you have an immediate knowledge that a crow is a bird, without ever experiencing one.

Evolutionary psychology takes a novel approach to the problem. It says that there is an innate predisposition for certain types of learning. "Only small parts of the brain resemble a tabula rasa; this is true even for human beings. The remainder is more like an exposed negative waiting to be dipped into a developer fluid."

37

2.15 ANALYTIC–SYNTHETIC DISTINCTION

Immanuel Kant, in his *Critique of Pure Reason*, drew a distinction between "analytic" and "synthetic" propositions. He contended that some propositions are such that we can know them to be true just by understanding their meaning.

For example, consider, "My father's brother is my uncle." We can know it to be true solely by virtue of our understanding what its terms mean. Philosophers call such propositions "analytic." Synthetic propositions, on the other hand, have distinct subjects and predicates. An example of a synthetic proposition would be, "My father's brother has black hair."

Kant stated that all mathematical and scientific statements are synthetic a priori propositions because they are necessarily true but our knowledge about the attributes of the mathematical or physical subjects we can only get by logical inference.

The American philosopher W. V. O. Quine, in his "Two Dogmas of Empiricism", famously challenged the distinction, arguing that the two have a blurry boundary. Some contemporary philosophers have offered more sustainable accounts of the distinction.

3. TENDENCIES WITHIN EPISTEMOLOGY

3.1 HISTORICAL

The historical study of philosophical epistemology is the historical study of efforts to gain philosophical understanding or knowledge of the nature and scope of human knowledge.

Since efforts to get that kind of understanding have a history, the questions philosophical epistemology asks today about human knowledge are not necessarily the same as they once were.

But that does not mean that philosophical epistemology is itself a historical subject, or that it pursues only or even primarily historical understanding.

3.2 EMPIRICISM

In philosophy, empiricism is generally a theory of knowledge focusing on the role of experience, especially experience based on perceptual observations by the senses. Certain forms treat all knowledge as empirical, while some regard disciplines such as mathematics and logic as exceptions.

There are many variants of empiricism, positivism and realism being among the most commonly expounded but central to all empiricist epistemologies is the notion of the epistemologically privileged status of sense data.

3.3 IDEALISM

Many idealists believe that knowledge is primarily (at least in some areas) acquired by *a priori* processes or is innate—for example, in the form of concepts not derived from experience.

The relevant theoretical processes often go by the name "intuition". The relevant theoretical concepts may purportedly be part of the structure of the human mind (as in

39

Kant's theory of transcendental idealism), or they may be said to exist independently of the mind (as in Plato's theory of Forms).

3.4 RATIONALISM

By contrast with empiricism and idealism, which centres around the epistemologically privileged status of sense data (empirical) and the primacy of Reason (theoretical) respectively, modern rationalism adds a third 'system of thinking', (as Gaston Bachelard has termed these areas) and holds that all three are of equal importance: The empirical, the theoretical and the *abstract*. For Bachelard, rationalism makes equal reference to all three systems of thinking.

3.5 CONSTRUCTIVISM

Constructivism is a view in philosophy according to which all "knowledge is a compilation of human-made constructions", "not the neutral discovery of an objective truth". Whereas objectivism is concerned with the "object of our knowledge", constructivism emphasises "how we construct knowledge".

Constructivism proposes new definitions for knowledge and truth that form a new paradigm, based on inter-subjectivity instead of the classical objectivity, and on viability instead of truth.

Piagetian constructivism, however, believes in objectivity—constructs can be validated through experimentation. The constructivist point of view is pragmatic; as Vico said: "The norm of the truth is to have made it."

40

3.6 REGRESS PROBLEM, THE

"... to justify a belief one must appeal to a further justified belief. This means that one of two things can be the case.

Either there are some [epistemologically basic] beliefs that we can be justified for holding, without being able to justify them on the basis of any other belief, or else for each justified belief there is an infinite regress of (potential) justification [the nebula theory].

On this theory there is no rock bottom of justification. Justification just meanders in and out through our network of beliefs, stopping nowhere."

The apparent impossibility of completing an infinite chain of reasoning is thought by some to support scepticism. Socrates said, "The only true wisdom is in knowing you know nothing."

3.7 RESPONSE TO THE REGRESS PROBLEM

Many epistemologists studying justification have attempted to argue for various types of chains of reasoning that can escape the regress problem.

3.8 INFINITISM

It is not impossible for an infinite justificatory series to exist. This position is known as "infinitism". Infinitists typically take the infinite series to be merely potential, in the sense that an individual may have indefinitely many reasons available to him, without having consciously thought through all of these reasons when the need arises.

This position is motivated in part by the desire to avoid what is seen as the arbitrariness and circularity of its chief competitors, foundationalism and coherentism.

In mathematics, an infinite series will sometimes converge – (this is the basis of calculus) – one can therefore have an infinite series of logical arguments and analyse it for a convergent (or non-convergent) solution.

3.9 FOUNDATIONALISM

Foundationalists respond to the regress problem by asserting that certain "foundations" or "basic beliefs" support other beliefs but do not themselves require justification from other beliefs.

These beliefs might be justified because they are self-evident, infallible, or derive from reliable cognitive mechanisms. Perception, memory, and a priori intuition are often considered to be possible examples of basic beliefs.

The chief criticism of foundationalism is that if a belief is not supported by other beliefs, accepting it may be arbitrary or unjustified, though foundationalism is based upon the principle that these beliefs are infallible enough to be recognised as such in practice.

3.10 COHERENTISM

Another response to the regress problem is coherentism, which is the rejection of the assumption that the regress proceeds according to a pattern of linear justification.

To avoid the charge of circularity, coherentists hold that an individual belief is justified circularly by the way it fits together (coheres) with the rest of the belief system of which it is a part.

This theory has the advantage of avoiding the infinite regress without claiming special, possibly arbitrary status for some particular class of beliefs.

Yet, since a system can be coherent while also being wrong, coherentists face the difficulty of ensuring that the whole system corresponds to reality.

Additionally, most logicians agree that any argument that is circular is trivially valid. That is, to be illuminating, arguments must be linear with conclusions that follow from stated premises.

However, Warburton writes in 'Thinking from A to Z,' "Circular arguments are not invalid; in other words, from a logical point of view there is nothing intrinsically wrong with them. However, they are, when viciously circular, spectacularly uninformative. (Warburton 1996)."

3.11 FOUNDHERENTISM

A position known as "foundherentism", advanced by Susan Haack, is meant to be a unification of foundationalism and coherentism. One component of this theory is what is called the "analogy of the crossword puzzle."

Whereas, for example, infinitists regard the regress of reasons as "shaped" like a single line, Susan Haack has argued that it is more like a crossword puzzle, with multiple lines mutually supporting each other.

What do people know? At the heart of the question is scepticism, with many approaches involved trying to disprove some particular form of it.

3.12 SCEPTICISM

Scepticism is related to the question of whether certain knowledge is possible. If point B cannot be proven before point A, and if in order to prove point A it must be established with absolute certainty, then scepticism argues that it is difficult to prove any point at all. Sceptics argue that the belief in something does not necessarily justify an assertion of knowledge of it.

In this sceptics oppose foundationalism, which states that there have to be some basic beliefs that are justified without reference to others. The sceptical response to this can take several approaches.

First, claiming that "basic beliefs" must exist, amounts to the logical fallacy of argument from ignorance combined with the slippery slope. While a foundationalist would use Münchhausen trilemma as a justification for demanding the validity of basic beliefs, a sceptic would see no problem with admitting the result.

3.13 DEVELOPMENTS FROM SCEPTICISM

Early in the 20th century, the notion that belief had to be justified as such to count as knowledge lost favour. Fallibilism is the view that knowing something does not entail certainty regarding it. Charles Sanders Peirce was a fallibilist and the most developed form of fallibilism can be traced to Karl Popper (1902–1994) whose first book *Logik Der Forschung* (*The Logic of Scientific Discovery*), 1934 introduced a "conjectural turn" into the philosophy of science and epistemology at large.

He adumbrated a school of thought that is known as Critical Rationalism with a central tenet being the rejection of the idea that knowledge can ever be justified in the strong form that is sought by most schools of thought. His two most helpful exponents are the late William W Bartley and David Miller, recently retired from the University of Warwick.

3.14 EPISTEMIC CULTURE

Epistemic culture distinguishes between various settings of knowledge production and stresses their contextual aspects. Coined by Karin Knorr-Cetina in her book *Epistemic Cultures*; she defines epistemic cultures as an "amalgam of arrangements and mechanisms—bonded through affinity, necessity and historical coincidence—which in a given field, make up how we know what we know".

The term provides the conceptual framework used to demonstrate that different laboratories do not share the same "scientific" knowledge production model, but rather each is endowed with a different epistemic culture prescribing what adequate knowledge is and how it is obtained. Since its introduction, the term has been picked up and used by various researchers engaging in science and technology studies.

45

4.   KNOWLEDGE AND JUSTIFIED BELIEF

4.1 NARROW DEFINITION

Defined narrowly, epistemology is the study of knowledge and justified belief.

As the study of knowledge, epistemology is concerned with the following questions:

- What are the necessary and sufficient conditions of knowledge?

- What are its sources?

- What is its structure, and what are its limits?

As the study of justified belief, epistemology aims to answer questions such as:

- How we are to understand the concept of justification?

- What makes justified beliefs justified?

- Is justification internal or external to one's own mind?

Understood more broadly, epistemology is about issues having to do with the creation and dissemination of knowledge in particular areas of inquiry.

4.2 SOURCES OF KNOWLEDGE AND JUSTIFICATION

Beliefs arise in people for a wide variety of causes. Among them, we must list psychological factors such as desires, emotional needs, prejudice, and biases of various kinds.

Obviously, when beliefs originate in sources like these, they don't qualify as knowledge even if true. For true beliefs to count as knowledge, it is necessary that they originate in sources we have good reason to consider reliable.

46

These are perception, introspection, memory, reason, and testimony.

4.3 PERCEPTION (AS IN PHILOSOPHY)

Our perceptual faculties are our five senses: sight, touch, hearing, smelling, and tasting. We must distinguish between an experience that can be classified as *perceiving* that *p* (for example, seeing that there is coffee in the cup and tasting that it is sweet), which entails that *p* is true, and a perceptual experience in which it seems to us as though *p*, but where *p* might be false.

The reason for making this distinction lies in the fact that perceptual experience is fallible. The world is not always as it appears to us in our perceptual experiences. We need, therefore, a way of referring to perceptual experiences in which *p* seems to be the case that allows for the possibility of *p* being false.

That is the role assigned to perceptual seemings. So some perceptual seemings that *p* are cases of perceiving that *p*, others are not.

When it looks to you as though there is a cup of coffee on the table and in fact there is, the two states coincide. If, however, you hallucinate that there is a cup on the table, you have perceptual seeming that *p* without perceiving that *p*.

One family of epistemological issues about perception arises when we concern ourselves with the psychological nature of the perceptual processes through which we acquire knowledge of external objects. According to *direct realism*, we can acquire such knowledge because we can directly perceive such objects.

For example, when you see a tomato on the table, *what you perceive* is the tomato itself. According to *indirect realism*, we

47

acquire knowledge of external objects by virtue of perceiving something else, namely appearances or sense-data.

An indirect realist would say that, when you see and thus know that there is a tomato on the table, what you really see is not the tomato itself but a tomato-like sense-datum or some such entity.

Direct and indirect realists hold different views about the structure of perceptual knowledge. Indirect realists would say that we acquire perceptual knowledge of external objects by virtue of perceiving sense data that represent external objects.

Sense data, a species of mental states, enjoy a special status: we know directly what they are like. So, indirect realists think that, when perceptual knowledge is foundational, it is knowledge of sense data and other mental states. Knowledge of external objects is indirect: derived from our knowledge of sense data.

The basic idea is that we have indirect knowledge of the external world because we can have foundational knowledge of our own mind. Direct realists can be more liberal about the foundation of our knowledge of external objects. Since they hold that perceptual experiences get you in direct contact with external objects, they can say that such experiences can give you foundational knowledge of external objects.

We take our perceptual faculties to be reliable. But how can we know that they are reliable? For externalists, this might not be much of a challenge. If the use of reliable faculties is sufficient for knowledge, and if by using reliable faculties we acquire the belief that our faculties are reliable, then we come to know that our faculties are reliable. But even externalists might wonder how they can, via argument, *show* that our perceptual faculties are reliable.

The problem is this. It would seem the only way of acquiring knowledge about the reliability of our perceptual faculties is through memory, through remembering whether they served us well in the past. But should I trust my memory, and should I think that the episodes of perceptual success that I seem to recall were in fact episodes of perceptual success?

If I am entitled to answer these questions with 'yes', then I need to have, to begin with, reason to view my memory and my perceptual experiences as reliable. It would seem, therefore, that there is no non-circular way of arguing for the reliability of one's perceptual faculties.

4.4 INTROSPECTION

Introspection is the capacity to inspect the, metaphorically speaking, "inside" of one's mind. Through introspection, one knows what mental states one is in: whether one is thirsty, tired, excited, or depressed.

Compared with perception, introspection appears to have a special status. It is easy to see how a perceptual seeming can go wrong: what looks like a cup of coffee on the table might be just be a clever hologram that is visually indistinguishable from an actual cup of coffee.

But could it be possible that it introspectively seems to me that I have a headache when in fact I do not? It is not easy to see how it could be. Thus we come to think that introspection has a special status. Compared with perception, introspection seems to be privileged by virtue of being less error prone. How can we account for the special status of introspection?

First, it could be argued that, when it comes to introspection, there is no difference between appearance and reality; therefore, introspective seemings are necessarily successful introspections.

49

According to this approach, introspection is infallible. Alternatively, one could view introspection as a source of certainty. Here the idea is that an introspective experience of *p* eliminates all possible doubt as to whether *p* is true.

Finally, one could attempt to explain the special-ness of introspection by examining the way we respond to first-person reports: typically, we attribute a special authority to such reports. According to this approach, introspection is incorrigible. Others are not, or at least not typically, in a position to correct first-person reports of one's own mental states.

Introspection reveals how the world appears to us in our perceptual experiences. For that reason, introspection has been of special interest to foundationalists. Perception is not immune to error.

If certainty consists in the absence of all possible doubt, perception fails to yield certainty. Hence beliefs based on perceptual experiences cannot be foundational. Introspection, however, might deliver what we need to find a firm foundation for our beliefs about external objects: at best outright immunity to error or all possible doubt, or perhaps more modestly, an epistemic kind of directness that cannot be found in perception.

Is it really true, however, that, compared with perception, introspection is in some way special? Critics of foundationalism have argued that introspection is certainly not infallible. Might one not confuse an unpleasant itch for a pain? Might I not think that the shape before me appears circular to me when in fact it appears slightly elliptical to me? If it is indeed possible for introspection to mislead, then it is hard to see why introspection should eliminate all possible doubt.

Yet it is not easy to see either how, if one clearly and distinctly feels a throbbing headache, one could be mistaken about that. Introspection, then, turns out to be a mysterious faculty. On the one hand, it does not seem to be in general an infallible faculty; on the other hand, when looking at appropriately described specific cases, error does seem impossible.

4.5 MEMORY

Memory is the capacity to retain knowledge acquired in the past. What one remembers, though, need not be a past event. It may be a present fact, such as one's telephone number, or a future event, such as the date of the next elections. Memory is, of course, fallible. Not every instance of taking oneself to remember that p is an instance of actually remembering that p. We should distinguish, therefore, between remembering that p (which entails the truth of p) and *seeming* to remember that p (which does not entail the truth of p).

One issue about memory concerns the question of what distinguishes memorial seemings from perceptual seemings or mere imagination. Some philosophers have thought that having an image in one's mind is essential to memory, but that would appear to be mistaken. When one remembers one's telephone number, one is unlikely to have an image of one's number in one's mind.

The distinctively epistemological questions about memory are these: First, what makes memorial seemings a source of justification? Is it a necessary truth that, if one has a memorial seeming that p, one has thereby prima facie justification for p? Or is memory a source of justification only if, as coherentists might say, one has reason to think that one's memory is reliable? Or is memory a source of justification only if, as externalists would say, it is in fact reliable? Second, how can we respond to scepticism about knowledge of the past? Memorial seemings of the past do not guarantee that the past is what we take it to be.

We think that we are a bit older than just five minutes, but it is logically possible that the world sprang into existence just five minutes ago, complete with our dispositions to have memorial seemings of a more distant past and items such as apparent fossils that suggest a past going back millions of years. Our seeming to remember that the world is older than a mere five minutes does not entail, therefore, that it really is. Why, then, should we think that memory is a source of knowledge about the past?

4.6 REASON

Some beliefs would appear to be justified solely by the use of reason. Justification of that kind is said to be *a priori*: prior to any kind of experience. A standard way of defining *a priori* justification goes as follows:

A Priori Justification

S is justified *a priori* in believing that *p* if and only if *S*'s justification for believing that *p* does not depend on any experience.

Beliefs that are true and justified in this way would count as instances of *a priori* knowledge.

What exactly counts as experience? If by 'experience' we mean just *perceptual* experiences, justification deriving from introspective or memorial experiences would count as *a priori*.

For example, I could then know *a priori* that I'm thirsty, or what I ate for breakfast this morning. While the term '*a priori*' is sometimes used in this way, the strict use of the term restricts *a priori* justification to justification derived *solely* from the use of reason.

52

According to this usage, the word 'experience' includes perceptual, introspective, and memorial experiences. On this narrower understanding, paradigm examples of what I can know on the basis of *a priori* justification are conceptual truths (such as "All bachelors are unmarried"), and truths of mathematics, geometry and logic.

Justification and knowledge that is not *a priori* is called '*a posteriori*' or 'empirical'. For example, in the narrow sense of '*a priori*', whether I am thirsty or not is something I know empirically (on the basis of introspective experiences), whereas I know *a priori* that 12 divided by 3 is 4.

Several important issues arise about *a priori* knowledge.

First, does it exist at all? Sceptics about *apriority* deny its existence. They don't mean to say that we have no knowledge of mathematics, geometry, logic, and conceptual truths. Rather, what they claim is that all such knowledge is empirical.

Second, if *a priori* justification is possible, exactly how does it come about? What *makes* a belief such as "All bachelors are unmarried" justified solely on the basis of reason? Is it an unmediated grasp of the truth of this proposition? Or does it consist of grasping that the proposition is *necessarily* true? Or is it the purely intellectual experience of "seeing" (with they "eye of reason") or "intuiting" that this proposition is true (or necessarily true)? Or is it, as externalists would suggest, the reliability of the cognitive process by which we come to recognize the truth of such a proposition?

Third, if *a priori* knowledge exists, what is its extent? *Empiricists* have argued that *a priori* knowledge is limited to the realm of the *analytic*, consisting of propositions of a somehow inferior status because they are not really "about the world". Propositions of a superior status, which convey

53

genuine information about world, are labelled *synthetic*. *a priori* knowledge of synthetic propositions, empiricists would say, is not possible. *Rationalists* deny this. They would say that a proposition such as "If a ball is green all over, then it doesn't have black spots" is synthetic and knowable *a priori*.

A fourth question about the nature of *a priori* knowledge concerns the distinction between necessary and contingent truths. The received view is that whatever is known *a priori* is necessarily true, but there are epistemologists who disagree with that.

4.7 TESTIMONY

Testimony differs from the sources we considered above because it is not distinguished by having its own cognitive faculty. Rather, to acquire knowledge of *p* through testimony is to come to know that *p* on the basis of someone's saying that *p*. "Saying that *p*" must be understood broadly, as including ordinary utterances in daily life, postings by bloggers on their web-logs, articles by journalists, delivery of information on television, radio, tapes, books, and other media.

So, when you ask the person next to you what time it is, and he/she tells you, and you thereby come to know what time it is, that's an example of coming to know something on the basis of testimony. When you learn by reading the *Washington Post* that the terrorist attack in Sharm el-Sheikh of July 22, 2005 killed at least 88 people, that, too, is an example of acquiring knowledge on the basis of testimony.

The epistemological puzzle testimony that it raises is this: Why is testimony a source of knowledge? An externalist might say that testimony is a source of knowledge if and only if it comes from a reliable source. But here, even more so than in the case of our faculties, internalists will not find that answer satisfactory.

Suppose you hear someone saying '*p*'. Suppose further that a person is in fact utterly reliable with regard to the question of whether *p* is the case or not. Finally, suppose you have no evidential clue whatever as to that person's reliability. Would it not be plausible to conclude that, since that person's reliability is unknown to you, that person's saying '*p*' does not put you in a position to know that *p*? But if the reliability of a testimonial source is not sufficient for making it a source of knowledge, what else is needed?

Thomas Reid suggested that, by our very nature, we accept testimonial sources as reliable and tend to attribute credibility to them unless we encounter special contrary reasons. But that is merely a statement of the attitude we in fact take toward testimony. What is it that makes that attitude reasonable? It could be argued that, in one's own personal experiences with testimonial sources, one has accumulated a long track record that can be taken as a sign of reliability.

However, when we think of the sheer breadth of the knowledge we derive from testimony, one wonders whether one's personal experiences constitute an evidence base rich enough to justify the attribution of reliability to the totality of the testimonial sources one tends to trust.

An alternative to the track record approach would be to declare it a necessary truth that trusts in testimonial sources is justified. This suggestion, alas, encounters the same difficulty as the externalist approach to testimony: it does not seem we can acquire knowledge from sources the reliability of which is utterly unknown to us.

4.8 VIRTUE EPISTEMOLOGY

Epistemology, as commonly practiced, focuses on the subject's beliefs. Are they justified? Are they instances of knowledge? When it comes to assessing how the subject herself is doing with regard to the pursuit of truth and the seeking of

55

knowledge, this assessment is carried out by looking at the epistemic quality of her beliefs.

According to virtue epistemology, the order of analysis ought to be reversed. We need to begin with the subject herself and assess her epistemic virtues and vices: her "good" and her "bad" ways of forming beliefs. Careful and attentive reasoning would be an example of an epistemic virtue; jumping to conclusions would be an example of an epistemic vice.

It is only *after* we have determined which ways of forming beliefs count as epistemic virtues that we can, as a second step, determine the epistemic quality of particular beliefs. Its proponents construe virtue epistemology more or less stringently. According to pure virtue epistemology, epistemic virtues and vices are *sui generis*. They cannot be analysed in terms of more fundamental epistemic or non-epistemic concepts.

Proponents of a less stringent approach disagree with this; they would say that epistemic virtues and vices can fruitfully be analysed by employing other concepts. Indeed, according to an externalist strand of virtue epistemology, it is the very notion of reliability that we should employ to capture the difference between epistemic virtues and vices.

Stable ways of forming beliefs are epistemic virtues if and only if they tend to result in true beliefs, epistemic vices if and only if they tend to result in false beliefs. Virtue epistemology, thus conceived, is a form of reliabilism.

4.9 NATURALISTIC EPISTEMOLOGY

According to an extreme version of naturalistic epistemology, the project of traditional epistemology, pursued in an *a priori* fashion from the philosopher's armchair, is completely misguided. The "fruits" of such activity are demonstrably

56

false theories such as foundationalism, as well as endless and arcane debates in the attempt to tackle questions to which there are no answers. To bring epistemology on the right path, it must be made a part of the natural sciences and become cognitive psychology.

The aim of naturalistic epistemology thus understood is to *replace* traditional epistemology with an altogether new and redefined project. According to a moderate version of naturalistic epistemology, one primary task of epistemology is to identify how knowledge and justification are anchored in the natural world, just as it is the purpose of physics to explain phenomena like heat and cold, or thunder and lightning in terms of properties of the natural world.

The pursuit of this task does not require of its proponents to replace traditional epistemology. Rather, this moderate approach accepts the need for *cooperation* between traditional conceptual analysis and empirical methods. The former is needed for the purpose of establishing a conceptual link between knowledge and reliability, the latter for figuring out which cognitive processes are reliable and which are not.

4.10 RELIGIOUS EPISTEMOLOGY

In the history of philosophy, there are several famous arguments for the existence of God: the ontological argument, the cosmological argument, and the argument from design. From an epistemological point of view, the question is whether such arguments can constitute a rational foundation of faith, or even give us knowledge of God. A further question is whether, if God exists, knowledge of God might not also be possible in other ways, for example, on the basis of perception or perhaps mystical experiences.

There is also a famous problem casting doubt on the existence of God: Why, if God is an omniscient, omnipotent, and benevolent being, is there evil in the world? Here, the

57

epistemological question is whether, based on this problem, we can know that God (thus conceived) does not exist. Another, central issue for religious epistemology is raised by evidentialism. According to evidentialism, knowledge requires adequate evidence.

However, there does not seem to be any adequate evidence of God's existence. Is it possible, then, for theists to endorse evidentialism?

4.11 MORAL EPISTEMOLOGY

The basic moral categories are those of right and wrong action. When we do theoretical ethics, we wish to find out what it is that makes a right action right and a wrong action wrong. When we do practical or applied ethics, we attempt to find out which actions are right and which are wrong. The epistemological question these areas of philosophy raise is this: How can we *know* any of that?

Traditionally, philosophers have attempted to answer the questions of ethics via intuition, *a priori* reasoning, and the consideration of hypothetical cases. Some philosophers who belong to the naturalistic camp consider this approach misguided because they think that it is unreliable and liable to produce results that merely reflect our own cultural and social biases.

Among those who think that moral knowledge can be acquired via intuition and *a priori* reasoning, a primary question is whether the kind of justification such methods can generate is coherentist or foundationalist.

Finally, a further important question is whether moral knowledge is at all possible. Knowledge requires truth and thus objective reality. According to anti-realists, there is no objective reality of, and thus no truth about, moral matters. Since what is known must be true, it is not easy to see how, if

58

anti-realism were correct, there could be knowledge of moral matters.

4.12 SOCIAL EPISTEMOLOGY

When we conceive of epistemology as including knowledge and justified belief as they are positioned within a particular social and historical context, epistemology becomes social epistemology. How to pursue social epistemology is a matter of controversy. According to some, it is an extension and reorientation of traditional epistemology with the aim of correcting its overly individualistic orientation.

According to others, social epistemology ought to amount to a radical departure from traditional epistemology, which they see, like the advocates of radical naturalisation, as a futile endeavour.

Those who favour the former approach retain the thought that knowledge and justified belief are essentially linked to truth as the goal of our cognitive practices. They hold that there are objective norms of rationality that social epistemologists should aspire to articulate. Those who prefer the more radical approach would reject the existence of objective norms of rationality.

Moreover, since many view scientific facts as social constructions, they would deny that the goal of our intellectual and scientific activities is to find facts. Such constructivism, if weak, asserts the epistemological claim that scientific theories are laden with social, cultural, and historical presuppositions and biases; if strong, it asserts the metaphysical claim that truth and reality are themselves socially constructed.

4.13 FEMINIST EPISTEMOLOGY

When construed in a non-controversial way, the subject matter of feminist epistemology consists of issues having to do with fair and equal access of women to, and their participation in, the institutions and processes through which knowledge is generated and transmitted. Viewed this way, feminist epistemology can be seen as a branch of social epistemology.

When we move beyond this initial characterisation, what feminist epistemology is will become a matter of controversy. According to some, it includes the project of studying and legitimising special ways in which only women can acquire knowledge.

According to others, feminist epistemology should be understood as aiming at the political goal of opposing and rectifying oppression in general and the oppression of women in particular. At the extreme end, feminist epistemology is closely associated with post-modernism and its radical attack on truth and the notion of objective reality.

5. EPISTEMOLOGICAL LITERATURE

5.1 LIMITS OF HUMAN KNOWLEDGE.

Nearly every great philosopher has contributed to the epistemological literature. Some historically important issues in epistemology are whether:

> (1) Knowledge of any kind is possible, and if so what kind;

> (2) Some human knowledge is innate (i.e., present, in some sense, at birth) or whether instead all significant knowledge is acquired through experience;

> (3) Knowledge is inherently a mental state;

> (4) Certainty is a form of knowledge; and

> (5) The primary task of epistemology is to provide justifications for broad categories of knowledge claim or merely to describe what kinds of things are known and how that knowledge is acquired.

Issues related to (1) arise in the consideration of scepticism, radical versions of which challenge the possibility of knowledge of matters of fact, knowledge of an external world, and knowledge of the existence and natures of other minds

5.2 STUDY OF KNOWLEDGE

Epistemology is the branch of philosophy that studies knowledge. It attempts to answer the basic question: what distinguishes true (adequate) knowledge from false (inadequate) knowledge?

Practically, this question translates into issues of scientific methodology: how can one develop theories or models that are better than competing theories? It also forms one of the pillars of the new sciences of cognition, which developed from

61

the information processing approach to psychology, and from artificial intelligence, as an attempt to develop computer programs that mimic a human's capacity to use knowledge in an intelligent way.

When we look at the history of epistemology, we can discern a clear trend, in spite of the confusion of many seemingly contradictory positions. The first theories of knowledge stressed its absolute, permanent character, whereas the later theories put the emphasis on its relativity or situation-dependence, its continuous development or evolution, and its active interference with the world and its subjects and objects. The whole trend moves from a static, passive view of knowledge towards a more and more adaptive and active one.

Let us start with the Greek philosophers. In Plato's view knowledge is merely an awareness of absolute, universal *Ideas* or *Forms*, existing independent of any subject trying to apprehend to them. Though Aristotle puts more emphasis on logical and empirical methods for gathering knowledge, he still accepts the view that such knowledge is an apprehension of necessary and universal principles.

Following the Renaissance, two main epistemological positions dominated philosophy: *empiricism*, which sees knowledge as the product of sensory perception, and *rationalism* which sees it as the product of rational reflection.

5.3 REFLECTION-CORRESPONDENCE THEORY

The implementation of empiricism in the newly developed experimental sciences led to a view of knowledge which is still explicitly or implicity held by many people nowadays: the reflection-correspondence theory.

According to this view knowledge results from a kind of mapping or reflection of external objects, through our sensory organs, possibly aided by different observation instruments, to our brain or mind.

Though knowledge has no *a priori* existence, like in Plato's conception, but has to be developed by observation, it is still absolute, in the sense that any piece of proposed knowledge is supposed to either truly correspond to a part of external reality, or not.

In that view, we may in practice never reach complete or absolute knowledge, but such knowledge is somehow conceivable as a limit of ever more precise reflections of reality.

5.4 RATIONALISM AND EMPIRICISM

The following important theory developed in that period is the *Kantian synthesis* of rationalism and empiricism. According to Kant, knowledge results from the organization of perceptual data on the basis of inborn cognitive structures, which he calls "categories". Categories include space, time, objects and causality.

This epistemology does accept the subjectivity of basic concepts, like space and time, and the impossibility to reach purely objective representations of things-in-themselves. Yet the *a priori* categories are still static or given.

The next stage of development of epistemology may be called *pragmatic*. Parts of it can be found in early twentieth century approaches, such as logical positivism, conventionalism, and the "Copenhagen interpretation" of quantum mechanics. This philosophy still dominates most present work in cognitive science and artificial intelligence.

According to pragmatic epistemology, knowledge consists of models that attempt to represent the environment in such a way as to maximally simplify problem-solving.

It is assumed that no model can ever hope to capture all relevant information, and even if such a complete model would exist, it would be too complicated to use in any practical way. Therefore we must accept the parallel existence of different models, even though they may seem contradictory. The model which is to be chosen depends on the problems that are to be solved.

The basic criterion is that the model should produce correct (or approximate) predictions (which may be tested) or problem-solutions, and be as simple as possible. Further questions about the "Ding an Sich" or ultimate reality behind the model are meaningless.

5.5 PRAGMATICS

The pragmatic epistemology does not give a clear answer to the question where knowledge or models come from. There is an implicit assumption that models are built from parts of other models and empirical data on the basis of trial-and-error complemented with some heuristics or intuition. A more radical point of departure is offered by *constructivism.*

It assumes that all knowledge is built up from scratch by the subject of knowledge. There are no 'givens', neither objective empirical data or facts, nor inborn categories or cognitive structures. The idea of a correspondence or reflection of external reality is rejected. Because of this lacking connection between models and the things they represent, the danger with constructivism is that it may lead to relativism, to the idea that any model constructed by a subject is as good as any other and that there is no way to distinguish adequate or 'true' knowledge from inadequate or 'false' knowledge.

We can distinguish two approaches trying to avoid such an 'absolute relativism'. The first may be called individual constructivism. It assumes that an individual attempts to reach coherence among the different pieces of knowledge.

Constructions that are inconsistent with the bulk of other knowledge that the individual has will tend to be rejected.

Constructions that succeed in integrating previously incoherent pieces of knowledge will be maintained. The second, to be called social constructivism, sees consensus between different subjects as the ultimate criterion to judge knowledge. 'Truth' or 'reality' will be accorded only to those constructions on which most people of a social group agree.

In these philosophies, knowledge is seen as largely independent of a hypothetical 'external reality' or environment. As the 'radical' constructivists Maturana and Varela argue, the nervous system of an organism cannot in any absolute way distinguish between a perception (caused by an external phenomenon) and a hallucination (a purely internal event).

The only basic criterion is that different mental entities or processes within or between individuals should reach some kind of equilibrium.

Though these constructivistic approaches put much more emphasis on the changing and relative character of knowledge, they are still absolutist in the primacy they give to either social consensus or internal coherence, and their description of construction processes is quite vague and incomplete.

5.6 EVOLUTIONARY EPISTEMOLOGY

A more broad or synthetic outlook is offered by different forms or evolutionary epistemology. Here it is assumed that knowledge is constructed by the subject or group of subjects in order to adapt to their environment in the broad sense. That construction is an on-going process at different levels, biological as well as psychological or social.

65

Construction happens through blind variation of existing pieces of knowledge, and the selective retention of those new combinations that somehow contribute most to the survival and reproduction of the subject(s) within their given environment.

Hence we see that the 'external world' again enters the picture, although no objective reflection or correspondence is assumed, only an equilibrium between the products of internal variation and different (internal or external) selection criteria.

Any form of absolutism or permanence has disappeared in this approach, but knowledge is basically still a passive instrument developed by organisms in order to help them in their quest for survival.

A most recent, and perhaps most radical approach, extends this evolutionary view in order to make knowledge actively pursue goals of its own. This approach, which as yet has not had the time to develop a proper epistemology, may be called memetics. It notes that knowledge can be transmitted from one subject to another, and thereby loses its dependence on any single individual.

5.7 REPLICATED KNOWLEDGE

A piece of knowledge that can be transmitted or replicated in such a way is called a 'meme'. The death of an individual carrying a certain meme now no longer implies the elimination of that piece of knowledge, as evolutionary epistemology would assume.

As long as a meme spreads more quickly to new carriers, than that its carriers die, the meme will proliferate, even though the knowledge it induces in any individual carrier may be wholly inadequate and even dangerous to survival.

In this view a piece of knowledge may be successful (in the sense that it is common or has many carriers) even though its predictions may be totally wrong, as long as it is sufficiently 'convincing' to new carriers.

Here we see a picture where even the subject of knowledge has lost his primacy, and knowledge becomes a force of its own with proper goals and ways of developing itself. That this is realistic can be illustrated by the many superstitions, fads, and irrational beliefs that have spread over the globe, sometimes with a frightening speed.

Like social constructivism, memetics attracts the attention to communication and social processes in the development of knowledge, but instead of seeing knowledge as constructed by the social system, it rather sees social systems as constructed by knowledge processes. Indeed, a social group can be defined by the fact that all its members share the same meme (Heylighen, 1992).

Even the concept of 'self', that which distinguishes a person as a individual, can be considered as a piece of knowledge, constructed through social processes (HarrŽ, 19), and hence a result of memetic evolution.

From a constructivist approach, where knowledge is constructed by individuals or society, we have moved to a memetic approach, which sees society and even individuality as byproducts constructed by an ongoing evolution of independent fragments of knowledge competing for domination.

67

5.8 ANARCHISTIC, RELATIVISTIC ATTITUDE

We have come very far indeed from Plato's immutable and absolute Ideas, residing in an abstract realm far from concrete objects or subjects, or from the naive realism of the reflection-correspondence theory, where knowledge is merely an image of external objects and their relations.

At this stage, the temptation would be strong to lapse into a purely anarchistic or relativistic attitude, stating that 'anything goes', and that it would be impossible to formulate any reliable and general criteria to distinguish 'good' or adequate pieces of knowledge from bad or inadequate ones.

Yet in most practical situations, our intuition does help us to distinguish perceptions from dreams or hallucinations, and unreliable predictions ('I am going to win the lottery') from reliable ones ('The sun will come up tomorrow morning'). And an evolutionary theory still assumes a natural selection which can be understood to a certain degree.

Hence we may assume that it is possible to identify selection criteria, but one of the lessons of this historical overview will be that we should avoid to quickly formulate one absolute criterion. Neither correspondence, nor coherence or consensus, and not even survivability, are sufficient to ground a theory of knowledge. At this stage we can only hope to find multiple, independent, and sometimes contradictory criteria, whose judgment may quickly become obsolete.

Yet if we would succeed to formulate these criteria clearly, within a simple and general conceptual framework, we would have an epistemology that synthesizes and extends al of the traditional and less traditional philosophies above.

6. EPISTEMOLOGY: CORE AREA OF PHILOSOPHY

6.1 NATURE, SOURCES AND LIMITS

Epistemology is one of the core areas of philosophy. It is concerned with the nature, sources and limits of knowledge.

Epistemology has been primarily concerned with propositional knowledge, that is, knowledge that such-and-such is true, rather than other forms of knowledge, for example, knowledge how to such-and-such.

There is a vast array of views about propositional knowledge, but one virtually universal presupposition is that knowledge is true belief, but not mere true belief. For example, lucky guesses or true beliefs resulting from wishful thinking are not knowledge.

Thus, a central question in epistemology is: what must be added to true beliefs to convert them into knowledge?

6.2 FOUNDATIONALISM AND COHERENTISM

The historically dominant tradition in epistemology answers that question by claiming that it is the quality of the reasons for our beliefs that converts true beliefs into knowledge.

When the reasons are sufficiently cogent, we have knowledge. This is the normative tradition in epistemology. An analogy with ethics is useful: just as an action is justified when ethical principles sanction holding it.

The second tradition in epistemology, the naturalistic tradition, does not focus on the quality of the reasons for beliefs but, rather, requires that the conditions in which beliefs are acquired typically produce true beliefs.

Within the normative tradition, two views about the proper structure of reasons have been developed: foundationalism and coherentism.

By far, the most commonly held view is foundationalism. It holds that reasons rest on a foundational structure comprised of 'basic' beliefs. The foundational propositions have autonomous justification that does not depend upon any further justification which could be provided by inferential relations to other propositions.

These basic beliefs can be of several types. Empiricists (such as Hume and Locke) hold that basic beliefs exhibit knowledge initially gained through the senses or introspection

Rationalists (such as Descartes, Leibniz and Spinoza) hold that at least some basic beliefs are the result of rational intuition.

Since not all knowledge seems to be based on sense experience or introspection or rational intuition, some epistemologists claim that some knowledge is innate.

Still others argue that some propositions are basic in virtue of conversational contextual features.

Foundationalists hold that epistemic principles of inference are available that allows an epistemic agent to reason from the basic propositions to the non-basic (inferred) propositions. They suggest, for example, that if a set of basic propositions is explained by some hypothesis and additional confirming evidence for the hypothesis is discovered, then the hypothesis is justified

A notorious problem with this suggestion is that it is always possible to form more than one hypothesis that appears equally well confirmed by the total available data, and consequently no one hypothesis seems favoured over all its rivals.

Some epistemologists have argued that this problem can be overcome by appealing to features of the rival hypotheses beyond their explanatory power. For example, the relative simplicity of one hypothesis might be thought to provide a basis for preferring it to its rivals.

In contrast to foundationalism, coherentism claims that every belief derives its justification from inferential relationships to other beliefs.

All coherentists hold that, like the poles of a tepee, beliefs are mutually reinforcing. Some coherentists, however, assign a special justificatory role to those propositions that are more difficult to dislodge from the web of belief. The set of these special propositions overlaps the set of basic propositions specified by foundationalism.

There are some objections aimed specifically at foundationalism and others aimed specifically at coherentism. But there is one deep difficulty with both traditional normative accounts. This problem, known as the 'Gettier Problem' (after a famous three-page article by Edmund Gettier in 1963), can be stated succinctly as follows.

Suppose that a false belief can be justified, and suppose that its justificatory status can be transferred to another proposition through deduction or other principles of inference. Suppose further that the inferred proposition is true. If these suppositions can be true simultaneously - and that seems to be the case - the inferred proposition would be true, justified (by either foundationalist or coherentist criteria) and believed, but in many cases it clearly is not knowledge, since it is a felicitous coincidence that the truth was obtained.

71

One strategy for addressing the Gettier Problem remains firmly within the normative tradition. It employs the original normative intuition that it is the quality of the reasons which distinguishes knowledge from mere true belief. This is the defeasibility theory of knowledge. There are various defeasibility accounts but, generally, all of them hold that the felicitous coincidence can be avoided if the reasons which justify the belief are such that they cannot be defeated by further truths.

6.3 THE NATURALISTIC ANSWERS: CAUSES OF BELIEF

There is a second general strategy for addressing the Gettier Problem that falls outside of the normative tradition and lies squarely within the naturalistic tradition. As the name suggests, the naturalistic tradition describes knowledge as a natural phenomenon occurring in a wide range of subjects.

Adult humans may employ reasoning to arrive at some of their knowledge, but the naturalists are quick to point out that children and adult humans arrive at knowledge in ways that do not appear to involve any reasoning whatsoever. Roughly, when a true belief has the appropriate causal history, then the belief counts as knowledge.

Suppose that I am informed by a reliable person that the temperature outside the building is warmer now than it was two hours ago. That certainly looks like a bit of knowledge gained and there could be good reasons provided for the belief. The normativists would appeal to those good reasons to account for the acquisition of knowledge. The naturalists, however, would argue that true belief resulting from testimony from a reliable source is sufficient for knowledge.

Testimony is just one reliable way of gaining knowledge. There are other ways such as sense perception, memory and reasoning. Of course, sometimes these sources are faulty. A central task of naturalized epistemology is to characterize conditions in which reliable information is obtained. Thus, in some of its forms, naturalized epistemology can be seen as a branch of cognitive psychology, and the issues can be addressed by empirical investigation.

Now let us return to the Gettier Problem. Recall that it arose in response to the recognition that truth might be obtained through a felicitous coincidence. The naturalistic tradition ties together the belief and truth conditions of knowledge in a straightforward way by requiring that the means by which the true belief is produced or maintained should be reliable.

6.4 SCEPTICISM

The contrast between normative and naturalized epistemology is apparent in the way in which each addresses one of the most crucial issues in epistemology, namely, scepticism. Scepticism comes in many forms. In one form, the requirements for knowledge become so stringent that knowledge becomes impossible, or virtually impossible, to obtain. For example, suppose that a belief is knowledge only if it is certain, and a belief is certain only if it is beyond all logically possible doubt. Knowledge would then become a very rare commodity.

Other forms of scepticism only require that knowledge be based upon good, but not logically unassailable, reasoning. We have alluded to scepticism about induction. That form of scepticism illustrates the general pattern of the sceptical problem: there appear to be intuitively clear cases of the type of knowledge questioned by the sceptic, but intuitively plausible general epistemic principles appealed to by the sceptic seem to preclude that very type of knowledge.

Another example will help to clarify the general pattern of the sceptical problem. Consider the possibility that my brain is not lodged in my skull but is located in a vat and hooked up to a very powerful computer that stimulates it to have exactly

73

the experiences, memories and thoughts that I am now having. Call that possibility the 'sceptical hypothesis'. That hypothetical situation is clearly incompatible with the way I think the world is.

Now, it seems to be an acceptable normative epistemic principle that if I am justified in believing that the world is the way I believe it to be (with other people, tables, governments and so on), I should have some good reasons for denying the sceptical hypothesis.

But, so the argument goes, I could not have such reasons; for if the sceptical hypothesis were true, everything would appear to be just as it now does. So, there appears to be a conflict between the intuition that we have such knowledge and the intuitively appealing epistemic principle. Thus, scepticism can be seen as one instance of an interesting array of epistemic paradoxes.

Of course, epistemologists have developed various answers to scepticism. Within the normative tradition, there are several responses available. One of them is simply to deny any epistemic principle - even if it seems initially plausible - that precludes us from having what we ordinarily think is within our ken.

Another response is to examine the epistemic principles carefully in an attempt to show that, properly interpreted; they do not lead to scepticism. Of course, there is always the option of simply declaring that we do not have knowledge. Whatever choice is made, some initially plausible intuitions will be sacrificed.

Within the naturalistic tradition, there appears to be an easy way to handle the sceptical worries. Possessing knowledge is not determined by whether we have good enough reasons for our beliefs but, rather, whether the processes that produced the beliefs in question are sufficiently reliable. So, if I am a brain in a vat, I do not have knowledge; and if I am not a brain in a vat (and the world is generally the way I think it is), then I do have knowledge.

Nevertheless, those within the normative tradition will argue that we are obliged to withhold full assent to propositions for which we have less than adequate reasons, regardless of the causal history of the belief.

Contextualism, mentioned earlier, responds to the sceptical problem in a way that does not fall neatly into either the normative or naturalistic tradition. There are many varieties of contextualism, but central to all of them is that the truth conditions of a sentence or utterance attributing knowledge to someone will vary from one context to another.

Hence, the utterance `Sarah knows that the car she left in the parking lot is still there' will be true in one context when the standards for knowledge are lower than they are in a context in which the standards are those approaching certainty. In such a high standards context, Sarah will fail to know.

Thus, by extension, says the contextualist, both our ordinary claims to knowledge and the sceptical claims that we don't have knowledge can be true because of variations in the contexts of the utterances. So-called `invariantists' deny that there is such a contextual shift of the truth values of the utterances and, hence, they reject the contextualist solution to the sceptical problem.

6.5 RECENT DEVELOPMENTS IN EPISTEMOLOGY

Some recent developments in epistemology question and/or expand on some aspects of the tradition. Virtue epistemology focuses on the characteristics of the knower rather than individual beliefs or collections of beliefs.

Roughly, the claim is that when a true belief is the result of the exercise of intellectual virtue, it is, ceteris paribus, knowledge. Thus, the virtue epistemologist can incorporate certain features of both the normative and naturalist traditions.

Virtues, as opposed to vices, are good, highly prized dispositional states. The intellectual virtues, in particular, are just those deep dispositions that produce mostly true beliefs.

Such an approach reintroduces some neglected areas of epistemology, for example, the connection of knowledge to wisdom and understanding.

In addition, there are emerging challenges to certain presuppositions of traditional epistemology. For example, some argue that there is no set of rules for belief acquisition that are appropriate for all peoples and all situations.

Others have suggested that many of the proposed conditions of good reasoning, for example 'objectivity' or 'neutrality', are not invoked in the service of gaining truths, as traditional epistemology would hold, but rather they are employed to prolong entrenched power and (at least in some cases) distort the objects of knowledge.

In spite of these fundamental challenges and the suggestions inherent in some forms of naturalized epistemology that the only interesting questions are empirically answerable, it is clear that epistemology remains a vigorous area of inquiry for the natural sciences and social studies, at the heart of philosophy.

7. SUMMING UP

7.1 EVALUATIONS

The study of knowledge is one of the most fundamental aspects of philosophical inquiry. Any claim to knowledge must be evaluated to determine whether or not it indeed constitutes knowledge. Such an evaluation essentially requires an understanding of what knowledge is and how much knowledge is possible.

Defined narrowly, epistemology is the study of knowledge and justified belief. As the study of knowledge, epistemology is concerned with the following questions:

- What are the necessary and sufficient conditions of knowledge?

- What are its sources?

- What is its structure, and what are its limits?

As the study of justified belief, epistemology aims to answer questions such as:

- How we are to understand the concept of justification?

- What makes justified beliefs justified?

- Is justification internal or external to one's own mind?

Understood more broadly, epistemology is about issues having to do with the creation and dissemination of knowledge in particular areas of inquiry.

7.2 Anarchistic or Relativistic Attitudes

We have come very far indeed from Plato's immutable and absolute Ideas, residing in an abstract realm far from concrete objects or subjects, or from the naive realism of the reflection-correspondence theory, where knowledge is merely an image of external objects and their relations.

At this stage, the temptation would be strong to lapse into a purely anarchistic or relativistic attitude, stating that 'anything goes', and that it would be impossible to formulate any reliable and general criteria to distinguish 'good' or adequate pieces of knowledge from bad or inadequate ones.

Yet in most practical situations, our intuition does help us to distinguish perceptions from dreams or hallucinations, and unreliable predictions ('I am going to win the lottery') from reliable ones ('The sun will come up tomorrow morning').

An evolutionary theory still assumes a natural selection which can be understood to a certain degree. Hence we may assume that it is possible to identify selection criteria, but one of the lessons of this historical overview will be that we should avoid to quickly formulating one absolute criterion.

Neither correspondence, nor coherence or consensus, and not even survivability, are sufficient to ground a theory of knowledge. At this stage we can only hope to find multiple, independent, and sometimes contradictory criteria, whose judgment may quickly become obsolete.

Yet if we would succeed to formulate these criteria clearly, within a simple and general conceptual framework, we would have an epistemology that synthesises and extends all of the traditional and less traditional philosophies.

7.3 IMPORTANCE OF EPISTEMOLOGY

Epistemology is the explanation of how we think. It is required in order to be able to determine the true from the false, by determining a proper method of evaluation. It is needed in order to use and obtain knowledge of the world around us. Without epistemology, we could not think.

More specifically, we would have no reason to believe our thinking was productive or correct, as opposed to random images flashing before our mind. With an incorrect epistemology, we would not be able to distinguish truth from error.

The consequences are obvious. The degree to which our epistemology is correct is the degree to which we could understand reality, and the degree to which we could use that knowledge to promote our lives and goals.

Flaws in epistemology will make it harder to accomplish anything.

7.4 KEY ELEMENTS OF EPISTEMOLOGY

Our senses are valid, and the only way to gain information about the world. Reason is our method of gaining knowledge, and acquiring understanding. Logic is our method of maintaining consistency within our sets of knowledge.

Objectivity is our means of associating knowledge with reality to determine its validity. Concepts are abstracts of specific details of reality, or of other abstractions. A proper epistemology is a rational epistemology.

7.5 SYSTEMATIC OVERVIEW

This book attempts to provide a systematic overview of the epistemological problems that several questions may raise and focus in some depth on issues relating to the structure and the limits of knowledge and justification.

While this book provides an overview of the important issues, it of course leaves the most basic questions unanswered; as such epistemology will continue to be an ever expanding area of philosophical discussion as long as questions remain.

END

INDEX   PAGE

A PRIORI AND A POSTERIORI	*17*
ACQUIRING KNOWLEDGE	36
ANALYTIC PHILOSOPHY	12
ANALYTIC–SYNTHETIC DISTINCTION	38
ANARCHISTIC OR RELATIVISTIC ATTITUDES	78
ANARCHISTIC, RELATIVISTIC ATTITUDE	68
APPLICATION OF EPISTEMOLOGY	23
BACKGROUND AND MEANING	5
BELIEF	27
COHERENTISM	42
COMMON APPLICATIONS	23
CONSTRUCTIVISM	40
DEVELOPMENTS FROM SCEPTICISM	44
EDMUND GETTIER	29
EMPIRICISM	18
EMPIRICISM	39
EPISTEMIC CULTURE	45
EPISTEMOLOGICAL LITERATURE	61
EPISTEMOLOGY	9
EPISTEMOLOGY: CORE AREA OF PHILOSOPHY	69
EVALUATIONS	77
EVOLUTIONARY EPISTEMOLOGY	65
EXISTENTIALISM	15
EXTERNALISM AND INTERNALISM	33
FEMINIST EPISTEMOLOGY	60
FOUNDATIONALISM AND COHERENTISM	69
FOUNDATIONALISM	42
FOUNDHERENTISM	43
HEIDEGGER, MARTIN (1889-1976)	20
HISTORICAL	39
IDEALISM	39
IMPORTANCE OF EPISTEMOLOGY	79
INDIAN THOUGHT	21

INFALLIBILISM, INDEFEASIBILITY	31
INFINITISM	41
INTROSPECTION	49
JUSTIFICATION	28
KEY ELEMENTS OF EPISTEMOLOGY	79
KNOWLEDGE AND JUSTIFIED BELIEF	46
LIMITS OF HUMAN KNOWLEDGE	61
MEANING	5
MEMORY	51
METAPHYSICS	8
MORAL EPISTEMOLOGY	58
NARROW DEFINITION	46
NATIVISM	18
NATURALISTIC ANSWERS: CAUSES OF BELIEF	72
NATURALISTIC EPISTEMOLOGY	56
NATURE, SOURCES AND LIMITS	69
ONTOLOGY	20
PERCEPTION (AS IN PHILOSOPHY)	13
PERCEPTION	47
PHILOSOPHICAL THEORY OF KNOWLEDGE	10
PHILOSOPHY	5
PRACTICAL APPLICATIONS	23
PRAGMATICS	64
PRAGMATISM	15
PROPOSITIONAL KNOWLEDGE	26
PROPOSITIONS	29
RATIONALISM AND EMPIRICISM	63
RATIONALISM	17
RATIONALISM	40
REASON	52
RECENT DEVELOPMENTS IN EPISTEMOLOGY	75
REFLECTION-CORRESPONDENCE THEORY	62
REGRESS PROBLEM, THE	41
RELIABILISM	32
RELIGIOUS EPISTEMOLOGY	57
REPLICATED KNOWLEDGE	66

RESPONSE TO THE REGRESS PROBLEM 41
RESPONSES TO GETTIER 31
SCEPTICISM 16
SCEPTICISM 44
SCEPTICISM 73
SCIENCE, PHILOSOPHY OF 10
SOCIAL EPISTEMOLOGY 59
SOURCES OF KNOWLEDGE & JUSTIFICATION 46
STUDY OF KNOWLEDGE 61
SUBSTANCE 13
SUMMING UP 77
SYSTEMATIC OVERVIEW 80
TENDENCIES WITHIN EPISTEMOLOGY 39
TESTIMONY 54
TRUTH 27
VALUE PROBLEM, THE 35
VERIFICATIONISM (in philosophy) 19
VIRTUE EPISTEMOLOGY 55

BIBLIOGRAPHY

All books publications mentioned in this bibliography are written by Andreas Sofroniou

1. I.T. RISK MANAGEMENT, ISBN: 978-1-4467-5653-9
2. SYSTEMS ENGINEERING, ISBN: 978-1-4477-7553-9
3. BUSINESS INFORMATION SYSTEMS, CONCEPTS AND EXAMPLES, ISBN: 978-1-4092-7338-7
4. A GUIDE TO INFORMATION TECHNOLOGY, ISBN: 978-1-4092-7608-1
5. CHANGE MANAGEMENT IN I.T., ISBN: 978-1-4092-7712-5
6. FRONT-END DESIGN AND DEVELOPMENT FOR SYSTEMS APPLICATIONS, ISBN: 978-1-4092-7588-6
7. I.T RISK MANAGEMENT, ISBN: 978-1-4092-7488-9
8. I.T. RISK MANAGEMENT – 2011 EDITION, ISBN: 978-1-4467- 5653-9
9. THE SIMPLIFIED PROCEDURES FOR I.T. PROJECTS DEVELOPMENT, ISBN: 978-1-4092-7562-6
10. THE SIGMA METHODOLOGY FOR RISK MANAGEMENT IN SYSTEMS DEVELOPMENT, ISBN: 978-1-4092-7690-6
11. TRADING ON THE INTERNET IN THE YEAR 2000 AND BEYOND, ISBN: 978-1-4092- 7577
12. STRUCTURED SYSTEMS METHODOLOGY, ISBN: 978-1-4477-6610-0
13. INFORMATION TECHNOLOGY LOGICAL ANALYSIS, ISBN: 978-1-4717-1688-1
14. I.T. RISKS LOGICAL ANALYSIS, ISBN: 978-1-4717-1957-8
15. I.T. CHANGES LOGICAL ANALYSIS, ISBN: 978-1-4717-2288-2
16. LOGICAL ANALYSIS OF SYSTEMS, RISKS , CHANGES, ISBN: 978-1-4717-2294-3
17. COMPUTING, A PRÉCIS ON SYSTEMS, SOFTWARE AND HARDWARE, ISBN: 978-1-2910-5102-5
18. MANAGE THAT I.T. PROJECT, ISBN: 978-1-4717-5304-6
19. CHANGE MANAGEMENT, ISBN: 978-1-4457-6114-5
20. MANAGEMENT OF I.T. CHANGES, RISKS, WORKSHOPS, EPISTEMOLOGY, ISBN: 978-1-84753-147-6
21. THE MANAGEMENT OF COMMERCIAL COMPUTING, ISBN: 978-1-4092-7550-3
22. PROGRAMME MANAGEMENT WORKSHOP, ISBN: 978-1-4092-7583-1
23. THE PHILOSOPHICAL CONCEPTS OF MANAGEMENT THROUGH THE AGES, ISBN: 978-1-4092- 7554-1
24. THE MANAGEMENT OF PROJECTS, SYSTEMS, INTERNET, AND RISKS, ISBN: 978-1-4092- 7464-3
25. HOW TO CONSTRUCT YOUR RESUMÉ, ISBN: 978-1-4092-7383-7
26. DEFINE THAT SYSTEM, ISBN: 978-1-291-15094-0
27. INFORMATION TECHNOLOGY WORKSHOP, ISBN: 978-1-291-16440-4
28. CHANGE MANAGEMENT IN SYSTEMS, ISBN: 978-1-4457-1099-0

29. SYSTEMS MANAGEMENT, ISBN: 978-1-4710-4907-1
30. TECHNOLOGY, A STUDY OF MECHANICAL ARTS AND APPLIED SCIENCES, ISBN: 978-1-291-58550-6
31. EXPERT SYSTEMS, KNOWLEDGE ENGINEERING FOR HUMAN REPLICATION, ISBN: 978-1-291- 59509-3
32. ARTIFICIAL INTELLIGENCE AND INFORMATION TECHNOLOGY, ISBN: 978-1-291- 60445-0
33. PROJECT MANAGEMENT PROCEDURES FOR SYSTEMS DEVELOPMENT, ISBN: 978-0-952-72531-2
34. SURFING THE INTERNET, THEN, NOW, LATER. ISBN: 978-1--291-77653-9
35. ANALYTICAL DIAGRAMS FOR I.T. SYSTEMS, ISBN: 978-1-326-05786-2
36. INTEGRATION OF INFORMATION TECHNOLOGY, ISBN: 978-1-312-84303-1
37. MEDICAL ETHICS THROUGH THE AGES, ISBN: 978-1-4092- 7468-1
38. MEDICAL ETHICS, FROM HIPPOCRATES TO THE 21ST CENTURY ISBN: 978-1-4457-1203-1
39. THE MISINTERPRETATION OF SIGMUND FREUD, ISBN: 978-1-4467-1659-5
40. JUNG'S PSYCHOTHERAPY: THE PSYCHOLOGICAL & MYTHOLOGICAL METHODS, ISBN: 978-1-4477-4740-6
41. FREUDIAN ANALYSIS & JUNGIAN SYNTHESIS, ISBN: 978-1-4477-5996-6
42. ADLER'S INDIVIDUAL PSYCHOLOGY AND RELATED METHODS, ISBN: 978-1-291-85951-5
43. ADLERIAN INDIVIDUALISM , JUNGIAN SYNTHESIS, FREUDIAN ANALYSIS, ISBN: 978-1-291-85937-9
44. PSYCHOTHERAPY, CONCEPTS OF TREATMENT, ISBN: 978-1-291-50178-0
45. PSYCHOLOGY, CONCEPTS OF BEHAVIOUR, ISBN: 978-1-291-47573-9
46. PHILOSOPHY FOR HUMAN BEHAVIOUR, ISBN: 978-1-291-12707-2
47. SEX, AN EXPLORATION OF SEXUALITY, EROS AND LOVE, ISBN: 978-1-291-56931-5
48. PSYCHOLOGY FROM CONCEPTION TO SENILITY, ISBN: 978-1-4092-7218-2
49. PSYCHOLOGY OF CHILD CULTURE, ISBN: 978-1-4092-7619-7
50. JOYFUL PARENTING, ISBN: 0 9527956 1 2
51. THE GUIDE TO A JOYFUL PARENTING, ISBN: 0 952 7956 1 2
52. THERAPEUTIC PHILOSOPHY FOR THE INDIVIDUAL AND THE STATE, ISBN: 978-1-4092-7586-2
53. PHILOSOPHIC COUNSELLING FOR PEOPLE AND THEIR GOVERNMENTS, ISBN: 978-1-4092-7400-1
54. MORAL PHILOSOPHY, FROM SOCRATES TO THE 21ST AEON, ISBN: 978-1-4457-4618-0
55. MORAL PHILOSOPHY, FROM HIPPOCRATES TO THE 21ST AEON, ISBN: 978-1-84753-463-7
56. MORAL PHILOSOPHY, THE ETHICAL APPROACH THROUGH THE AGES, ISBN: 978-1-4092-7703-3
57. MORAL PHILOSOPHY, ISBN: 978-1-4478-5037-3
58. 2011 POLITICS, ORGANISATIONS, PSYCHOANALYSIS, POETRY, ISBN: 978-1-4467-

2741-6

59. PLATO'S EPISTEMOLOGY, ISBN: 978-1-4716-6584-4
60. ARISTOTLE'S AETIOLOGY, ISBN: 978-1-4716-7861-5
61. MARXISM, SOCIALISM & COMMUNISM, ISBN: 978-1-4716-8236-0
62. MACHIAVELLI'S POLITICS & RELEVANT PHILOSOPHICAL CONCEPTS, ISBN: 978-1-4716-8629-0
63. BRITISH PHILOSOPHERS, 16TH TO 18TH CENTURY, ISBN: 978-1-4717-1072-8
64. ROUSSEAU ON WILL AND MORALITY, ISBN: 978-1-4717-1070-4
65. HEGEL ON IDEALISM, KNOWLEDGE & REALITY, ISBN: 978-1-4717-0954-8
66. PHILOLOGY, CONCEPTS OF EUROPEAN LITERATURE, ISBN: 978-1-291-49148-7
67. THREE MILLENNIA OF HELLENIC PHILOLOGY, ISBN: 978-1-291-49799-1
68. CYPRUS, PERMANENT DEPRIVATION OF FREEDOM, ISBN: 978-1-291-50833-8
69. SOCIOLOGY, CONCEPTS OF GROUP BEHAVIOUR, ISBN: 978-1-291-51888-7
70. SOCIAL SCIENCES, CONCEPTS OF BRANCHES AND RELATIONSHIPS ISBN: 978-1-291-52321-8
71. CONCEPTS OF SOCIAL SCIENTISTS AND GREAT THINKERS, ISBN: 978-1-291-53786-4
72. THE TOWERING MISFEASANCE, ISBN: 978-1-4241-3652-0
73. DANCES IN THE MOUNTAINS – THE BEAUTY AND BRUTALITY, ISBN: 978-1-4092-7674-6
74. YUSUF'S ODYSSEY, ISBN: 978-1-291-33902-4
75. WILD AND FREE, ISBN: 978-1-4452-0747-6
76. HATCHED FREE, ISBN: 978-1-291-37668-5
77. THROUGH PRICKLY SHRUBS, ISBN: 978-1-4092-7439-1
78. BLOOMIN' SLUMS, ISBN: 978-1-291-37662-3
79. SPEEDBALL, ISBN: 978-1-4092-0521-0
80. SPIRALLING ADVERSARIES, ISBN: 978-1-291-35449-2
81. EXULTATION, ISBN: 978-1-4092-7483-4
82. FREAKY LANDS, ISBN: 978-1-4092-7603-6
83. MAN AND HIS MULE, ISBN: 978-1-291-27090-7
84. LITTLE HUT BY THE SEA, ISBN: 978-1-4478-4066-4
85. THE SAME RIVER TWICE, ISBN: 978-1-4457-1576-6
86. THE CANE HILL EFFECT, ISBN: 978-1-4452-7636-6
87. WINDS OF CHANGE, ISBN: 978-1-4452-4036-7
88. A TOWN CALLED MORPHOU, ISBN: 978-1-4092-7611-1
89. EXPERIENCE MY BEFRIENDED IDEAL, ISBN: 978-1-4092-7463-6
90. CHIRP AND CHAT (POEMS FOR ALL), ISBN: 978-1-291-75055-3
91. POETIC NATTERING, ISBN: 978-1-291-75603-6
92. SOFRONIOU COLLECTION OF FICTION BOOKS, ISBN: 978-1-326-07629-0
93. EPISTEMOLOGY, A SYSTEMATIC OVERVIEW, ISBN: 978-1-326-11380-3

www.ingramcontent.com/pod-product-compliance
Lightning Source LLC
Chambersburg PA
CBHW060438290526
45791CB00002B/988